THE CHURCH OF ENGLAND
AND THE CHURCH OF CHRIST

THE
CHURCH OF ENGLAND
AND THE
CHURCH OF CHRIST

BY

A. E. J. RAWLINSON, D.D.

ARCHDEACON OF AUCKLAND;
CANON RESIDENTIARY OF DURHAM CATHEDRAL;
LATE STUDENT AND TUTOR OF CHRIST CHURCH, OXFORD.

LONGMANS, GREEN AND CO.
LONDON ✤ NEW YORK ✤ TORONTO
1930

LONGMANS, GREEN AND CO. LTD.

39 PATERNOSTER ROW, LONDON, E.C.4
6 OLD COURT HOUSE STREET, CALCUTTA
53 NICOL ROAD, BOMBAY
MOUNT ROAD, MADRAS

LONGMANS, GREEN AND CO.

55 FIFTH AVENUE, NEW YORK
221 EAST 20TH STREET, CHICAGO
TREMONT TEMPLE, BOSTON
128-132 UNIVERSITY AVENUE, TORONTO

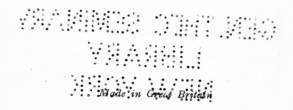

Made in Great Britain

To

The Right Reverend Father in God

HERBERT

by Divine Providence

Lord Bishop of Durham.

PREFACE

THE Church of England occupies at the present time a peculiar position. Theoretically the Church of the nation, it has an actual communicant roll of about one fourteenth of the population. Vague well-wishers, occasional worshippers, and nominal adherents are, of course, much more numerous ; and it is evident that recent discussions, both in the press and in Parliament, have had the effect of arousing a widely-extended public interest, even on the part of that large section of the nation which does not habitually share in the Church's corporate worship of God. The ' man in the street ' is prepared to take an interest in the Church of England ; and he has his own views of the Church.

Unfortunately they are not, as a rule, based upon knowledge. The affairs of a religious community, more particularly in respect of such matters as are concerned with its own inner spiritual life, its religious beliefs, and its system of corporate worship, are not really intelligible except from within. The majority of the people of England is not, it is to be feared, at the present time rightly to be regarded as being ' within ' the Church of England, in the sense and for the purposes indicated. It is, indeed, only too manifest that the Church has not in modern times succeeded in being, in any adequate sense, ' understanded of the people '.

It would moreover appear that, even of those who are actual and practising members of the Church, there are not a few who, at the present time, are perplexed. The question has been seriously raised whether the Church of England is, in the last resort, anything more than a religious, or quasi-religious, department of State. The Church claims, indeed, to be more than this—claims, as of inherent right, to be spiritually free, and in matters directly and admittedly spiritual to acknowledge no ultimate sovereignty beyond that of the Lord Jesus Christ. Is such a claim, in the case of an ' Established ' Church, justified ?

Again, the questions are asked : Does the Church of England possess genuine internal cohesion and unity ? Was not the late Bishop of Zanzibar in the right when he described it as having ' an exceedingly chaotic system of truth ' ? To what is the Anglican Church really committed in matters of doctrine, and for what does it stand ? Has it any intelligible *raison d'être* as a specific variant of the Christian

tradition in the midst of a Christendom which more
and more seeks after unity ?

The present short work is an attempt to answer
these questions. The writer has sought to recognize
and to state the facts fairly, and at the same time to
explain why it is that he believes in the Church of
England and in its future. The lecture form of the
chapters is due to the fact that, by invitation of the
President and Court of Governors of Sion College,
London, the substance of the book was delivered in
Lent as a course of four lectures to London clergy.
The fourth lecture has, since its delivery, been greatly
expanded, and parts of the earlier lectures have been
here and there modified and, in some cases, enlarged.
It is the writer's hope that the book, short as it is,
may contribute something towards making the
position of the Church of England better understood.

The Bishop of Durham has been kind enough to
accept the dedication, and to read the proofs of the
book. It must not, of course, be assumed that the
Bishop endorses without qualification all the particular views which it contains.

A. E. J. RAWLINSON.

The College,
        Durham,
            November, 1929.

CONTENTS

CHAPTER I

THE CHURCH OF CHRIST

I HAVE been invited to attempt to answer the question, 'What does the Church of England stand for?' In this first lecture I want to begin further back, and to invite you to consider not the Church of England as such, but the Church Universal, the Church of Christ and of God.

What do we mean by the term 'Church'? The idea is derived from the Bible, and in order to understand it, it is necessary to begin not with the New Testament, but with the Old: for the roots of the idea of the Church are to be found in the conception of Israel, the People of God. All early religion is intensely corporate and social: the early religion of the Hebrews, with which we are concerned in the earlier parts of the Old Testament, was no exception to this rule. God, we are told, made a 'covenant' with Abraham[1]: but by 'Abraham' is meant here the traditional progenitor of *the people of Israel;* and the 'covenant' is made with Abraham *and with his descendants.*[2] The 'covenant' thus made with 'Abraham' is sub-

[1] Gen. xv, 18.   [2] Gen. xvii, 1 *seqq.*

B

sequently renewed at Mount Sinai,[1] and the people of Israel becomes henceforward the People of God.

The great Old Testament prophets (we are sometimes informed) 'individualised' religion. They proclaimed certainly a doctrine of individual responsibility, and they were concerned very largely (though by no means exclusively) with the problems of what to-day would be called individual and personal religion. But the 'individual' with whom the prophets are concerned (and the fact is sometimes forgotten) is still the individual *Israelite*. What the prophets teach is that God looks to the heart. 'They are not all Israel' (so S. Paul subsequently expressed it) 'which are of Israel.'[2] As the prophets themselves put it, there was a distinction to be drawn between the righteous in Israel, and the unrighteous. The former, who alone were the true Israelites, might very well prove, and indeed *would* probably prove, to be no more than a 'remnant' of the actual Israel. They were nevertheless the 'elect' remnant, the nucleus of the true Israel, the ideal People of God of the future. The 'salvation' anticipated by the prophets was in no case the mere deliverance or escape of individuals, considered abstractly in isolation from one another or from Israel. On the contrary, what the prophets had

---

[1] Exod. xxiv, 3–8.   [2] Rom. ix, 6.

in mind was the social and corporate salvation of the elect ' remnant '—the purified and redeemed People of God. In this prophetic conception of the redeemed Israel we have presented to us already the fundamental idea of the Church.

The New Testament carries the thought further. Salvation is, in a measure, already at the New Testament stage actualised. The Church *is* the redeemed Israel—even though there is a sense also in which the Church looks still for completed and final redemption hereafter.[1] The boundaries of the Church are at the same time enlarged : the disciples, charged with the new message of salvation, are commissioned and ' sent ', not to Israel alone, but to ' all nations.'[2] The Church, therefore, as the Brotherhood of the Redeemed, becomes, in its Christian phase, universal. It is confined to no race, no particular people. It is a Society which is from henceforth super-racial, super-national, and (I would add) supernatural. Co-extensive, at least in idea and in principle (and potentially, therefore, in fact), with the whole of mankind as redeemed, it is the supreme Society of all.

I have called the Church ' supernatural ' : and I mean by that term that the Church does not

---

[1] Cf. (e.g.) Rom. viii, 18–25, and many other passages.
[2] Matt. xxviii, 19.

simply ' emerge ' in the merely natural course of world-history. On the contrary, the Church origi- nates in the creative activity and the redemptive purpose of God. It is in the world, but it does not derive its existence from the world. It belongs to the new order, the ' new creation ' of God. The Church, in the strict use of words, is not comparable to any mundane society. ' In the world ', but not ' of the world ',[1] as ' the people of God's own posses- sion ',[2] Christians ' have their existence ' (so an early writer expresses it) upon earth, but their ' citizen- ship ' is ' in heaven '.[3] The Church, that is to say, lives in the world, but her true life is elsewhere. She stands in relation, not merely to time, but to eternity ; and she lives with a supernatural life.

The New Testament does not think of the Lord Jesus Christ as having ' founded ' the Church, but as having redeemed it. The Church is the heir both of the patriarchs and of the promises,[4] and was ' in the wilderness ' with Moses.[5] The Church is the ' mystery which from all ages hath been hid in God, who created all things ',[6] and the faithful were ' chosen ' in Christ ' before the foundation of the world.'[7] There is a sense, not to be ignored, in

---

[1] John xvii, 11, 14, 16.   [2] 1 Pet. ii, 9.
[3] *Ep. ad Diognet*, v, 9 : cf. Philipp. iii, 20.
[4] Rom. ix, 4–5, with Eph. iii, 6.   [5] Acts vii, 38.
[6] Eph. iii, 9.   [7] Eph, i. 4.

which it may be affirmed that the People of God
has in Christ been reconstituted and created afresh ;
but the Church, as the true, the supernatural, or
the ' spiritual ' Israel, is in a most real sense continuous still with the ancient ' olive tree ' of the
Synagogue. There has been a ' casting away ' in
part of the old Israel, who had ' stumbled ' by reason
of unbelief ; and there has been a ' grafting in ' of
the Gentiles.[1] But the Church is still Israel—
S. Paul calls it ' the Israel of God ' ;[2] and its
members are citizens, chosen in Christ, of ' the
Jerusalem which is above.'[3] There is a passage,
indeed, in which S. Paul distinguishes the ' Church
of God ' both from the ' Jews ' and from the
' Greeks ' as a kind of third entity (the *genus tertium*
of later Christian Apologists) ;[4] and in the Fourth
Gospel the expression ' the Jews ' is used regularly to
denote those Jews who reject the Messiah. But from
the point of view of the New Testament, speaking
generally, the Church is so essentially Israel that
the Old Testament Scriptures are everywhere taken
over and interpreted so as to have reference not
merely to the Jewish, but to the Christian, *Ecclesia*.
They are the Scriptures no longer of the Synagogue,
but of the Church. It is to ' the elect who are

[1] Rom. xi, 15 ; ix, 32 *seq.* ; xi, 17 *seqq.*
[2] Gal. vi, 16.   Gal. iv, 26.
[4] I Cor. x, 32 : cf. Tertull, *Scorp.*, x, etc.

sojourners of the Dispersion in Pontus, Galatia,
Cappadocia, Asia and Bithynia '—that is to say (if
the phrase may be permitted) to the scattered
members of the ' Dispersion after the Spirit '—that
the writer of I Peter addresses the astonishing words
(every phrase of which is an echo of the Old Testament, and betokens the ascription to the Christian
Ecclesia of some one or another of the prerogatives
of Israel of old) : ' But ye are an elect race, a royal
priesthood, a holy nation, a people for God's own
possession, that ye may show forth the excellencies
of him who called you out of darkness into his
marvellous light : which in time past were no
people, but are now the people of God : which had
not obtained mercy, but now have obtained mercy.'[1]

The actual *word* ' Church ', or ἐκκλησία, (used in
the Acts, in one passage,[2] in its ordinary classical
sense as denoting the assembly of the citizens in
a Greek state), was not borrowed by Christianity
from secular usage, but was taken over from the
Greek of the Septuagint. The word had been used

[1] I Pet. ii, 9 *seq*. For the Old Testament echoes in the passage
see the references in the margin of any reference Bible. Note in
particular that the phrase ' royal priesthood ' (cf. Rev. i, 6 and
v, 10) is based on the description of Israel in Exod. xix, 6 : and
therefore it cannot be validly argued that the corporate ' priesthood ' of ' all believers ' which this passage affirms is in any way
incompatible, under the New Covenant any more than under
the Old, with the existence for certain purposes of a specific
ministerial ' priesthood ', *within* the ' royal ' and ' priestly '
community of the People of God as a whole.

[2] Acts xix, 39, 40.

by the Alexandrian translators of the Old Testament
to render one or other of the two Hebrew words
('*edah* and *kahal*) which in the original text stood
for the ' assembly ' or ' congregation ' of the people
of Israel.   The two words in question were *both*
rendered indiscriminately in the Septuagint by *either*
of the two Greek words συναγωγή (or ' synagogue ')
and ἐκκλησία (or ' Church ').   The word συναγωγή in
Hellenistic Jewish usage denoted either a place of
religious assembly (the actual synagogue building)
or the organized society of Jewish worshippers (the
local ' synagogue ' of Jews) who were accustomed
to meet there.   The word ἐκκλησία was not used, it
would seem, of a ' synagogue.'   It was a Septuagintal
synonym of συναγωγή which in ordinary usage does
not seem to have been taken over into the language
of every-day speech.   It retained, therefore, its
strict Biblical meaning, and denoted, not a particular
' synagogue ', but the whole stock of Israel, the
' assembly ' of which Scripture had spoken, the
' people of God ' as a whole.

It was in this sense that the word was adopted
by Christianity (that is to say, by the earliest *Greek*-
speaking Christianity) to denote the redeemed
' People of God ', the ἐκκλησία or ' Church ' of the
Messiah, the ' elect remnant ' of Israel.   The taking
over of this particular term from the Septuagint
was exceedingly easy.   It appears full grown, and

already familiar, in the Pauline Epistles. It is not
likely that S. Paul was the originator of it. Canon
Lacey has suggested that it was a conscious archaism,
based on the Scriptures : the term ' synagogue ' had
become degraded in common use, and the new Israel
required a distinctive title, expressive at once of its
difference from the synagogues of ' Israel after the
flesh ', and of its claim to identity with the Old
Testament ' Church '.[1]

It is not likely that the Lord Jesus Himself used
the Greek word ἐκκλησία.   If the substance (as
distinguished from the present Greek wording and
context) of the famous words to S. Peter in Matthew
xvi, 18 represents an authentic saying of His, the
reference is in all probability to the idea of the
' building up ' by the Messiah of the fallen ' taber-
nacle of David ' ; and the nucleus of the new Israel
which is to be ' built up ' is the elect Remnant of
the old, of which S. Peter, acknowledging the Christ,
is the first serviceable ' stone '.[2]

The word ἐκκλησία, or ' Church ', like the word
' synagogue ', can be used in the New Testament in
the plural—we hear of ' the churches of Judæa ',[3]
the ' seven churches of Asia ',[4] the ' churches of

---

[1] T. A. Lacey, *The One Body and the One Spirit*, pp. 19–25.
The above paragraphs are greatly indebted to Canon Lacey's
excellent and illuminating discussion.

[2] Lacey, *op. cit.*, pp. 32 *seq.* *Cf.* Ps. cxlvii, 2 ; Jer. xxiv, 6,
xxxi, 4, 28, xxxiii, 7, etc. ; also Acts xv, 15 *seqq.*

[3] Gal. i, 22.   [4] Rev. i, 4.

God ',[1] and ' all the churches '.[2] As so used, it
denotes not different ' denominations ' of Christians
—there were of course no such things, in New
Testament times, as ' denominations ', in the modern
sense of that term—but particular Christian ' assem-
blies ', particular localised ' churches ', each of which,
in its particular place (its particular city, or even
the ' house ' where its members customarily as-
sembled) was *the* ' Church ', the ἐκκλησία of God.
The thought of ' catholicity ' or universality (in the
sense of extension throughout the whole world) is
perhaps not yet explicit—the term ' Catholic ' as
applied to the Church is first found in the Epistles
of S. Ignatius of Antioch, probably about A.D. 110.[3]
There is nevertheless reason to believe that the
religious sense of the term ' Church ', as denoting
the elect ' People of God ', is historically prior (as it
is in any case logically prior) to the merely empirical
sense in which the word can be used to denote a
particular concrete and local ἐκκλησία. To have
affirmed the priority of the religious sense of the
term ' Church ', and by consequence the priority of
the whole ' Church '—the whole ' people of God '—
to the scattered empirical ' churches ', has been the

---

[1] 1 Cor. xi, 16.   [2] 1 Cor. vii, 17 ; 2 Cor. viii, 18 ; xi, 28.
[3] *Cf.* Ignat. *ad Smyrn.*, viii, 2 ; ὅπου ἂν φανῇ ὁ ἐπίσκοπος,
ἐκεῖ τὸ πλῆθος ἔστω, ὥσπερ ὅπου ἂν ᾖ Χριστὸς Ἰησοῦς, ἐκεῖ
ἡ καθολικὴ ἐκκλησία.

service rendered in modern times by the German Lutheran writer, Rudolf Sohm, the author of *Kirchenrecht*. ' Two that sit together and are occupied in the words of the Law ' (so runs a Jewish saying) ' have the Shechinah (i.e. the Divine Presence) among them.'[1] The New Testament ascribes a similar saying to our Lord.[2] *Ubi Christus, ibi ecclesia ;* and so also *ubi tres, ibi ecclesia*—where ' two or three ' are gathered together in the Name of Christ, there is the Church : not a particular ' church ', but the Church as such, the one redeemed Israel of God, locally manifested in space and in time.

After this long introduction we begin, then, with the idea of the Church as the redeemed People of God, described in the New Testament as ' the Church of the firstborn who are enrolled in heaven ',[3] or again as Israel ' after the Spirit '.[4] The Church or ' People ' of the living God, at once old and new, *ecclesia militans, expectans, triumphans,* ' the blessed company of all faithful people ', the mystical ' Body ' of the ' Christ '—that is what, in the first instance, we ought to mean by the ' Church '. No less majestic and no narrower conception is in any way adequate ; and if I have laboured this point, it is because there is a real danger in modern times of a weakened or depotentiated sense of the word

[1] *Pirke Aboth*, iii, 3.   [2] Matt. xviii, 20.
[3] Heb. xii, 23.   [4] *Cf.* Gal. iv, 22 *seqq.*

' Church ', comparable to the depotentiated sense of
the word ' synagogue ' in the Judaism of Hellenistic
times. A modern scholar, a lay convert to Romanism,
writes with bitter sarcasm that " the term ' Church '
is often used in the North of Europe and in the
United States of America to denote a club of persons
combining to hire and employ what the Greeks
would have called a *sophist* to lecture to them on
moral and literary topics."[1] It is an unfair carica-
ture even of the most depotentiated and secularised
types of modern protestant religion : but the
exaggeration does certainly draw attention to a
peril. A Church is not a religious club ; and in the
deepest sense of its meaning the word ' Church ' has
no plural. There is one ' Church ', and there is *only*
one ' Church ', because there is only one God, and
by consequence only one People of God ; and the
Church, the redeemed ' Israel of God ', is in the
ultimate grounds of her being a Society not of this
world. She is *one*, and she is *holy*, and she is *catholic*
(in the sense of being universal). The Church is also
apostolic—and that is a word which has the effect of
bringing us immediately to earth.

The Church is apostolic, in the first place, in the
sense of being *missionary :* she is the Society which

[1] J. S. Phillimore, *Philostratus : In honour of Apollonius of
Tyana,* I, p. xiii.

has been put in trust with the Gospel, as God's revealed message for mankind ; the Society, therefore, which is charged with an universal mission— ' Go ye into all the world '.[1] The Church is, in the second place, apostolic in the sense of being *authoritative :* she is the inheritor, *for the purposes of her mission*, of a spiritual ' authority ' which, if it derives, in a certain sense, from the ' Apostles ' (who were ' sent ' by Christ as the Messiah), derives originally, through Christ, from *God* (by whom Christ Himself was ' sent ' into the world).[2] It is precisely this temporal mission of the Church, this note of ' apostolicity ', which has the effect, as I have said, of bringing us immediately to earth. A Church which is ' sent ' into the world to make disciples is clearly no merely abstract idea, no simply invisible entity of which the ' pattern ' (as Plato would say) is ' laid up in heaven ', but a visible and concrete Society, outwardly manifested in this actual world in which we live and move and in this life have our existence as concrete beings of flesh and blood.

Now, there is a distinction, familiar to Protestantism, and characteristic, perhaps, more especially of Lutheran Protestantism (though it is by no means

[1] Mark xvi, 15 ; *cf*. Matt. xxviii, 19.
[2] John xx, 21.

confined to the Lutherans), between the *ecclesia visibilis* and the *ecclesia invisibilis*, between the ' invisible ' and the ' visible ' Church. The ' invisible Church ', it is maintained, which alone is, in the strict sense, the true and real Church, the Church glorious without spot or wrinkle or any such thing, is discerned and known only by faith, is indeed, in the strict sense, known only to God. The Church visible, as a society of actual men and women upon earth, is to be distinguished sharply from the Church in the strict, ultimate sense, the ' invisible ' Church of the redeemed. The two are related, of course ; but they are also distinguishable, and to be distinguished, from one another. As I once heard a Lutheran theologian expound it, there is a distinction to be drawn between the Church as the *creation*, and the Church as the *instrument*, of the Spirit. The Church is, from one point of view, an historical growth within history, an actual, concrete, and visible society ; and in the Church, thus regarded, institutionalism and externals, rites, sacraments, visible membership, and so forth, are inevitable. But the Church, at the same time, is super-historical, the direct creation of the Word: and we must recognise the freedom of God to choose as He will. He may, and does normally, utilise the visible Church as His instrument ; and God is free to use even a corrupt Church—He can even through

formalism and a merely outward proclamation of the
Word convert souls. But there is not always the
Spirit present in the Church as an institution : and
it is at all times possible for the ' visible Church ' in
a particular locality or period to become apostate,
so as to be in effect the instrument, no longer of
Christ, but of Anti-Christ. And God can raise up a
new organisation, a new ' visible Church ', to be the
instrument of His grace. It would be in this way,
I take it, that the traditional theology of the Lutheran
Church would account for what happened at the
time of the Reformation, after the excommunication
of Luther himself by the apostate ' harlot of Baby-
lon '. Between the Church as a *societas externa*, the
Church visible, and the Church as the *societas sancti
spiritus in cordibus*, the Church as the fellowship of
the Holy Spirit in Christian hearts, there is, from
the Lutheran point of view, a continuous, and in
practice an inevitable, tension. Nevertheless, though
(according to this theology) there is tension between
the two, and a distinction to be drawn always
between the ' invisible ' and the ' visible ' Church,
the opposition of the two is not absolute. They are
in the last resort rather, ideally speaking, two sides
or two aspects of one and the same Church. What
is practically meant (so my Lutheran friend explained
to me) by the doctrine of the ' invisibility ' of the

Church was that one could only *believe*, one could not, in the strict sense, *know*, that a particular person, or a particular assembly of persons, however ostensibly Christian, belonged to the true Church. There was tension, and inevitable tension, between the two ideas ; but on the other hand it was not right simply to acquiesce in this fact. It was the duty of Christians to seek to bring it about that the Church as visible should coincide or overlap with the ' Kingdom ', or Church as invisible. But this ideal, nevertheless, could never at any stage be achieved perfectly before the coming of the End, and the Judgment. The identification of the Church (in the sense of any particular manifestation of the Church visible) with the Kingdom—the insistence that the visible should coincide with the invisible— was of the essence of sectarianism.

Thus far my Lutheran friend. It will be obvious that in the last sentences he had the Church of Rome more particularly in view. I spoke at an earlier stage of this lecture of Rudolf Sohm. For Sohm also the starting-point of his theory of the Church is the Lutheran idea of the *ecclesia invisibilis*. The Church, in the spiritual and religious sense, he maintains, is invisible, but it was confused with the visible Church : and Catholicism (by which term Sohm means primarily *Latin* Catholicism) was born of the confusion.   For the Church, in so far as it exists as a *visible* society, must exist necessarily in a particular form, and must develop for itself rules, organisation, institutions, and eventually law.   If the visible, empirical Church is to be simply identified with the Church in the religious, or ' invisible ', sense, then the authority behind all these things is directly and without qualification divine.   The Church in the ' visible ' sense becomes identified with the ' ark of salvation ' ; and since there can only be one ' ark of salvation ', there can be only one visible Church, to which it is the indispensable duty of all Christians both to conform and to belong.   The conclusion is the Roman conclusion ; and, upon such a view, the excommunication, for example, of Luther meant that the latter was cut off from the Church. The excommunication of Luther—this particular historical case—appears indeed vitally to have affected and influenced the whole Lutheran theory of the Church : and the main reason, as I believe, why the Lutheran theologians cling still with such tenacity to the distinction between the ' invisible ' and the ' visible ' Church is that it appears to them to be religiously vital to be able to maintain that the excommunication of Luther did not mean that he was cast out from the Church in any sense that religiously mattered : he was merely cast out by the corrupt and apostate *ecclesia visibilis* of his day.

An adequate theology of the Church must no doubt cover all the facts ; but it does not follow from this that a theology devised primarily in order to account for exceptional cases will be the best type of theology. The rise, indeed, and the historical roots of the idea of the invisible Church (which, in the form at least in which it was maintained by the Reformers, whether Lutheran or Calvinist, was surely a novelty) are not difficult to explain.

(1) There was, in the first place, the Old Testament idea of the ' Remnant '—an idea, however, which in itself gives no justification to the theory of an ' *invisible* ' Church, since the ' Remnant ', though, no doubt, at any particular moment not easy to identify, is conceived in the Old Testament as an historical body, not as an invisible ' election '.

(2) There was, in the second place, the mixed moral experience of the Church, the discovery that the school of saints was the home also of sinners, and that there were ' unworthy members ' in the Body of Christ, a discovery which not unnaturally gave rise to the idea (we may recall more particularly the teaching of the Montanists and of Tertullian) that those who truly belonged to the Holy Church could not be simply identified with the visible body of the Church as a merely external society. But here,

C

again, there is nothing directly to justify the idea that the true Church is invisible, and known only to God.

(3) There was, in the third place, the idea of Predestination, characteristic more especially of the theology of S. Augustine, and taken over from the Augustinian tradition by the Reformers. The Church is ' the number of the elect ' (*numerus electorum*), and the elect of God are to be found (by a strange paradox) both inside and outside the Church ! ' In the ineffable fore-knowledge of God,' writes S. Augustine, ' many who appear to be without are within, and many who appear to be within are without.'[1] This conception, which, taken by itself, ' shatters ' (as Harnack remarks) ' every notion of the Church ',[2] was the result partly of S. Augustine's experience of conversion, and partly it was due to his exegesis of the ninth chapter of Romans. But in speaking of predestination, it is necessary to speak of the predestination not only of individuals, but also of the Church. God has chosen a holy people to represent Him in the world, and the new Israel is just as ' visible ' a society as the old. To maintain that the true Church is invisible is to evacuate the

---

[1] ' Namque in illa ineffabili præscientia dei multi qui foris videntur, intus sunt, et multi, qui intus videntur, foris sunt ' (Aug. *De Bapt.*, V, 38).

[2] Harnack, *History of Dogma*, E.T., V, p. 166.

doctrine of the vocation of the Church of its meaning.
The whole conception of the ' invisible Church ', in
the Lutheran and Calvinist sense, is simply unusable,
whether from the point of view of theology or from
the point of view of the practical pastor of souls.
At the most, or at best, it is a theory which is in-
voked at certain points as a *deus ex machina* to
explain certain difficulties. In Augustine's view, not
even the members themselves of the invisible Church
can be assured that they belong to it.[1] We can
simply say nothing about it ! In the Lutheran
presentations of the doctrine, the true Church is
perpetually tending to be regarded as invisible, while
yet at the same time the Church on earth is defined
as ' a congregation of faithful men, in which the pure
Word of God is preached, and the sacraments duly
administered.'[2] It is surely not possible to regard
either the preaching of the Word or the administration of the sacraments as being the functions of an
invisible Church ![3]

We reject, therefore, the Lutheran and Calvinist
distinction between the visible and the invisible

---

[1] Contrast the later Protestant doctrine of ' assurance.'

[2] The words of the Anglican Article XIX (' Of the Church ')
echo here almost verbally the definition of the Church in the
Augsburg Confession of 1530.

[3] The argument summarised in the text owes much to a speech
contributed by the Rev. Dr. J. K. Mozley to a theological discussion at Canterbury in April, 1927.

Church as being unsatisfactory. The Reformers were attempting to meet real difficulties ; but the sharp distinction which (with the help of the doctrine of Predestination) they were accustomed to draw between the Church as it appears outwardly upon earth and the true Church, as known only to God, has been the fruitful parent of schisms and sects, for the reason that it has consistently tended towards the relative religious disparagement of the Church as visibly organised. It has brought it about that, in the most characteristically Protestant circles, men have acquiesced with a light heart in the existence, side by side, of an indefinite plurality of visible Church bodies, each with its own specific rules, regulations, and laws, precisely on the ground that the rules, regulations and laws of the Church visible are, according to this view, in the last resort only of human and earthly significance. They exist as ordinances of the Church visible, because societies on earth must be organised, and a Church, considered as a society, possesses like other societies a natural right to make rules for its members. If a particular Church chooses to make itself narrow, it is within its rights in so doing : and the persons excluded may, if they choose, form a new Church of their own. There has been but little emphasis upon the conception of schism as a sin, and the members of a

plurality of competing Church bodies have all sung
cheerfully the words

> ' We are not divided,
> All one Body we '—

on the ground presumably that the faithful are all
inwardly united to Christ, but without any great
consciousness of paradox.

Nevertheless, though their solution of it was unsatisfactory, and the resulting chaos of sects and of
' Churches ' has been calamitous, the Reformers were
grappling with a genuine problem. A distinction
does need to be drawn between two meanings of the
word ' Church ', a distinction between the Church in
the ultimate sense, as the fellowship of the redeemed,
the Church glorious without spot or wrinkle or any
such thing, and the Church in the sense of the
Church visible and militant, a *mixtum corpus*, im-
perfect, marred by sins, rent asunder by schisms.

By the term ' schism ' is meant in this connexion
(and indeed it is the only intelligible meaning of the
term) an external division within Christendom,
marring the unity of the Church upon earth. Schism
is a bi-lateral relationship : it is a division within the
Christian body. Schismatics, unless they are also
apostates (i.e. unless they have ceased to be Christians at all), are not outside, but inside, the Church.
It is impossible for one body of Christians to be in

schism with another, even though it be with the main body, without the main body being also in schism with them.   It follows from this that the whole Church of Christ upon earth is at present in a condition of schism.   There is disunion, where there ought to be unity ; and we are involved, all of us, in greater degree or in less, in a common sin.   For we are in schism from our brethren.[1]

I would plead, then, for a distinction between the Church in the ultimate sense and the Church visible and militant on earth, but not for the Lutheran distinction, which with a light heart would justify schism.   The Church visible and militant on earth cannot and must not be simply distinguished, as merely earthly and human, from the Church as a religious idea.   The Church visible on earth, though it cannot indeed be simply identified *sans phrase* with the ultimate Church, nevertheless stands in an organic relationship towards it, as being both its temporal manifestation and the vehicle, here below, of its life.   It is divided by schisms and sects, but it ought not so to be divided.   It is in no sense a society, or group of societies, for which there are analogies of a valid kind in the political sphere.   It

---

[1] The best book on this subject is T. A. Lacey, *Unity and Schism* (The Bishop Paddock Lectures for 1917), published by A. R. Mowbray & Co.

is the Church of the living God upon earth—a conception of its nature which in principle excludes the sectarian idea.

There remains the problem of schism—Where is the true Church to be found? I have already indicated, in a broad sense, the answer; it is an answer to which, later on in the course of these lectures, we shall have to return. The Church visible and militant, which *ought* to be one, in actual fact is divided. But schism is a division within the Body, and the Church visible on earth is to be identified not with the Church of Rome, or with any particular Christian denomination in isolation, but with *Christendom, taken in a broad sense as a whole.*

There is a theory, of course, of the Church which would reckon as belonging to the true Body of Christ those great orthodox communions, and those only, which have preserved a technically valid episcopate, the Catholic creeds, and the Catholic sacraments. Even so, they are in schism from one another. ' We say ', remarks a recent author, ' that the Body has been divided by these schisms; but that is an awkward figure. If the Body had suffered the loss of its members by amputation, every one of its members would be dead, Rome as well as the others. We had better say that the Body is suffering from the curious and distracting trouble of dissociation, or multiple personality. Rome, in dissociation from the others, speaks and says, I am the real voice of the Body ; Constantinople, in dissociation from the others, speaks and says, I am the real voice of the Body ; Canterbury, in dissociation from the others, though it seems to claim a vague connection with Constantinople, speaks and says, I am the real voice of the Body. Rome speaks with a harsh and unsympathetic voice : Constantinople speaks with a venerable but wheezy voice ; Canterbury, too much of a multiple personality in itself, speaks with an intelligent but often a stuttering voice.'[1]

But there are other voices as well, the competing and various voices of the more definitely ' Protestant' Churches and sects. It is a mistake to ignore them. There may be defects of Church order, there may be weakness of sacramental life, there may even be a deficient grasp, in some cases, upon what are rightly regarded as fundamental doctrines of faith. Christendom is nevertheless wider than Rome, Canterbury, or Constantinople, taken separately or taken together ; and the plain man rightly feels that it is scandalous that we should be out of communion with *any* portion of Christendom. We shall have to accustom ourselves, in our thoughts about unity, to the habit of thinking, not simply in terms of the

---

[1] W. F. Stead, *The Shadow of Mount Carmel*, p. 169.

Latin, or of the Greek, or of the Anglican, or again of the more distinctively Evangelical and Protestant traditions, but in terms rather of Christendom.

A great deal of men's thought upon this subject has in the past been either sentimental, or archæological, or narrowly limited, or falsely legalistic, or sectarian, or in a variety of ways *doctrinaire*. We shall need to learn to think realistically, and to think also upon a sufficiently wide basis of actual knowledge. The facts of history must clearly be recognised. The facts—in so far as they are ascertainable—with regard to the historical beginnings of Church history are important. The facts of patristic and mediæval Church history are important no less. But so also are the facts of post-Reformation and modern Church history. The present needs to be understood in the whole light of the past, and it is only in the light of a profound and wide reading of history that the problems of to-day can be even confronted.

But there is at least no hope in any sectarian solution—Anglican, Roman, Evangelical, or Orthodox. The true inheritor of the Christendom of the past is not anything less than the whole complex and confused body of modern Christendom, as we know it to-day ; and the problem of Church Unity is as wide as the problem of Christendom.

CHAPTER II

OF the history of Christianity in England I do not propose to be so ambitious as to attempt even an outline. Celtic or pre-Roman Christianity, and the coming of S. Augustine, sent by the Pope, to Canterbury ; the Saxon Church, and the changes made by the Normans ; the dispute (familiar to canonists and to legal historians) as to whether, and (if so) during precisely what centuries, the Roman Canon Law was of force and validity in England ; the relations (varying in different periods) between English kings and Italian popes, and the rights and wrongs of their controversies—all these themes I must leave on one side. They are important ; but they are not important for the immediate purposes of this lecture. And their importance is sometimes exaggerated by those writers who desire to make controversial capital out of the past.

In particular, it is my own personal impression that by some schools of Anglican apologists too much has been made of the supposed latent nationalism of the English Church in the Middle Ages. The quarrels between Church and State, the resentment against Papal exactions, or against anything which suggested the idea of a foreign dominion in England, or of an usurpation of rights on the part of the Popes which were not constitutionally theirs, did not really mean that the *Ecclesia Anglicana* was in any sense even implicitly Protestant against the *religious* idea of the Papacy. On the contrary, the Church in England was, during the Middle Ages, definitely Roman, as well as Catholic—' an integral part of a Church which is described in the official language of English Bishops as Catholic, Apostolic and Roman.'[1] Reform came, and, as an incident therein, the repudiation of the Papacy ; but it is important to observe that the process of religious change did not follow in England the same lines which it had followed abroad. The history of the Reformation in England is a tangled and unsatisfactory affair. It is not necessary or desirable to idealise it, or, on the other hand, to ignore it. The task of the historian, here as elsewhere, is not to do either of these things, but to attempt to trace out and to understand the actual course of events.

There was a real sense in which the Church of England was protestantised. To the English Roman

[1] A. Hamilton Thompson in *Essays Catholic and Critical*, p. 350.

Catholic of the days of Elizabeth, just as much as to
the Romanist of to-day, the English Church was ' an
apostate communion to which the dignities of the
historic Church of the country had been transferred,
and its endowments, or such of them as had survived
the rapacity of the Crown and the court, had been
appropriated.'[1] I have been quoting from Professor
Hamilton Thompson's contribution to *Essays Catholic
and Critical*. I transcribe a few paragraphs more
from the same source.

There was much, as Professor Thompson points
out, to render plausible the Roman Catholic view.
' The traditional liturgy of the Church,' he writes,
' round which the fabric of mediæval faith had been
built and compacted, had gone with all its venerable
associations, and was banned as popish and super-
stitious. In its place there was a form of worship
which, if it had not entirely obliterated, at any rate
partially obscured its most familiar aspects, and was
celebrated with a bareness of ritual in strange
contrast with the solemnity of the ancient rite. The
process of denuding churches of all ornaments which
recalled the past went on under the direction of
prelates whose learning and love of antiquity were
somewhat inconsistent with their destructive zeal.

' Yet, amid all these changes, the old machinery

[1] A. Hamilton Thompson, *op. cit.*, p. 361.

of ecclesiastical government remained unimpaired
and in perfect working order. Within less than a
quarter of a century, four reigns had produced
startling fluctuations. Henry VIII had transferred
the papal authority over an orthodox Church to the
Crown. Under Edward VI the Church had been
protestantised. Mary brought it back into sub-
mission to Rome. Elizabeth deromanised it and
subjected it to interests of State. But, through all
this, the processes of ecclesiastical law had gone
forward in the old way. Apart from the changes of
constitution in certain cathedral churches consequent
upon the suppression of the monasteries, and from
the creation of a few new dioceses, there are few
alterations to be traced. The ordinary jurisdiction
of bishops remained as in the past. Officials and
vicars-general still exercised their delegated authority.
In the official records of English dioceses for this
period traces of contemporary change are few and
far between. Bishops were deprived of their sees
and burned for heresy, but the business of diocesan
administration, founded upon centuries of long
practice, was not interrupted for a single day. . . .

' More than this, in spite of the changes of *personnel*
among the bishops themselves, the episcopal succession was not visibly broken. It was preserved
throughout the reign of Edward VI at a time when

foreign non-episcopal bodies were gaining ground in
the country and novel systems had their best chance
of success. Without the maintenance of the episcopate, uniformity of religious practice was impossible :
the Church, split up into sects, would fall into
anarchy and become the prey of civil strife. Episcopacy formed the essential link with the past which
ensured order and discipline. It is possible that this,
which is not the highest view of the institution, was
the most powerful motive which influenced the filling
up in 1559 and 1560 of the sees vacant by the death
or deprivation of Marian bishops. Even so, the
consecration of new bishops was not undertaken
without the careful provision of valid means to
secure the historic continuity of the office.'[1]

And again,

' The preservation of episcopal order and jurisdiction, with the far-reaching consequences which it
involved, is the distinguishing feature of the English
Reformation. It had the inevitable effect of restoring
confidence, as time went on, to a Church distressed
by internal conflicts of opinion. The hold which
foreign protestantism had obtained upon the English
Church weakened throughout the Elizabethan period.
Puritan zealots found their cherished doctrines incompatible with episcopacy. In a primate like

---

[1] Hamilton Thompson, *op. cit.*, pp. 361, *seq.*

Whitgift, waging war on behalf of law and order, they saw an authority as dangerous to their ideals as any pope, and an authority backed by all the resources of civil government. For the stringent measures which the prelates of the sixteenth and seventeenth centuries employed against papists and puritans alike we can have little sympathy in an age of easy toleration. But it is impossible not to recognise that, with all the drawbacks to spirituality involved in the conditions of the Elizabethan settlement, the historic conception of the mission of the Church as the accredited guardian of the appointed means of divine grace held its own and steadily grew in strength. The position of a national Church, free from external interference, which Parker and Whitgift had used their power to uphold, was defined unmistakably by Laud and his supporters. In such men as Lancelot Andrewes, Jeremy Taylor, and George Herbert the power of the Church to attract and to nurture, through its ministry of the Word and Sacraments, the highest type of religious devotion was manifest. Loyal to the Reformation and recognising the protestant attitude of their Church to Rome, they yet proved that such loyalty was consistent with a theology and with forms of worship hallowed by antiquity, and justified the *via media* taken by the English Church as scriptural, primitive and truly Catholic.'[1]

Thus far Professor Hamilton Thompson. I have quoted his words as the best available summary in brief compass of the course actually taken by the Reformation in England. It is not an inspiring record. It is the story of a succession of varying changes and transformations, which were not so much desired *by* the Church, as determined *for* the Church by the policy of the civil government and the personal predilections of successive sovereigns. Continuity with the pre-Reformation Church the Professor is constrained to find primarily in the virtually unaltered functioning (apart, of course, from the abandonment of papal authority) of the outward fabric of Church government, and in the retention (for reasons mainly political, though in a form technically valid) of the episcopate and of the episcopal succession. The so-called ' settlement ' under Elizabeth—itself not final—was determined, only too obviously, by considerations of statecraft and policy. It was left for a later generation to justify *ex post facto* the *fait accompli*, to idealise Anglicanism, and to glorify in principle the *via media*.

Jewel wrote and published his *Apologia Ecclesiae Anglicanae* in 1562, and the first four books of

[1] *Op. cit.*, pp. 362 *seq.*

Hooker's *Laws of Ecclesiastical Polity* were published in 1594, before the death of Elizabeth ; but speaking broadly, it was not in the Tudor Age, but in the succeeding age of the Stuarts, that the great classical apologies for Anglicanism were produced. In the writings of men like Andrewes, Hooker, and Jeremy Taylor the position of the Church of England, as it had actually taken shape and was gradually coming to be understood, was defended with real learning and cogency (at least in relation to contemporary standards of knowledge and thought), and with a certain amount also of positive enthusiasm, as against both Rome and Geneva. It was not too soon, if the Church in its reformed guise was to appear to be anything more than a merely Erastian ' Establishment.' As Wakeman puts it, ' the work of Hooker, and Andrewes, and Jeremy Taylor was wanted to secure the results of the work of Elizabeth and Whitgift and Bancroft.'[1] But the work was done. A real theology of Anglicanism, or (to speak more precisely) an intellectual apologetic on behalf of the Anglican Church, was in being. And the Church of England, moreover, began to produce saints—men like Andrewes and Ken (who became Bishops), George Herbert (a parish priest in the country), and devout laymen like Nicholas Ferrar—who had been born

[1] H. O. Wakeman, *History of the Church of England*, p. 357.

D

and brought up in the reformed Church, who had been nurtured and trained in things spiritual by means of the religious practices of a distinctively Anglican type of piety, and who exhibited in life and in character the unmistakable fruits of the Spirit.

The Church of which these men were practising members was, whatever its demerits, at least an authentic manifestation of Christendom, a genuine organ of the Church Universal. In intention and theory (and to a considerable extent also in fact) it was the Church of the English people, continuous, in something more than a merely formal and constitutional sense, with its own past ; a Church, moreover, in which (notwithstanding local, and insular, and in certain respects temporary, peculiarities) the pure Word of God was proclaimed, and the sacraments duly administered.

It might be possible, then, to enquire : ' For what did the Church of England stand, at the stage in its development which had thus far been reached ? ' And it might be possible to reply : ' For the ideal of a Church which should be at once orthodox and national.'

Professor Brilioth, a learned and able continental observer, remarks of the English Church of the Reformation that it was primarily national. The policy of Elizabeth and of her advisers (he points out)

was an attempt—and a decidedly noteworthy
attempt—to include Christians of varying types and
of varying convictions within the fold of a single
nation-wide Church. Protestants (in the sense of
those who sympathised, in a general way, with the
Reformation) and Catholics (in the sense of those
who preferred rather the old ways, but who were
prepared to acquiesce in the Reform, and more
particularly in the breach with the Papacy) were
both alike to be included. ' But ' (remarks Dr.
Brilioth) ' the Protestantism which was thus com-
prehended ' (i.e. in the Church of England) ' was of
another type than the continental, and in comparison
with it thin and negative.'

What the Professor here means is that in the
initial stages of the Reformation in England there
was little of the positive warmth and enthusiasm
which marked what appeared to the Lutheran
Churches abroad to be a positively new illumination,
a rediscovery of the Gospel, as a free, liberating
message of divine grace and power, a transforming
word of ' good news ', to which the Church in
subjection to Rome had (as it was felt) done no kind
of adequate justice. ' Though Lutheran influence '
(the Professor writes) ' was not absent,' from the
earlier stages of the Reformation in England, ' yet
it was *to the early Fathers* that both Cranmer and

Ridley appealed in the last instance, and it was *by the standard of the primitive Church* that they designed to cut off the excrescences of Roman doctrine and cult. The English Reformation did not depend on any new spiritual awakening, and there was little experience of the violent religious crisis of the Continent, and the values which were its result.'[1]

It is true that a new and more powerful wave of reforming influence came by way of Frankfort and Zürich to England, a wave (this time) which was marked by a genuine enthusiasm ; but its sources of inspiration were Calvinist, rather than Lutheran ; and it arrived, moreover, too late. It affected a few of the leading Anglicans, more especially Bishop Jewel ; but it reached England after the main lines of the National Church in its new form were already laid down. It did not succeed in producing a revolution within the Church, or in working its will. What it did was to create an ecclesiastical opposition —it gave rise to that Puritan party against whom, on the ground of their persistent reluctance to conform, prelates like Whitgift and Bancroft contended, and in reply to whose criticisms of the existing Church system Hooker wrote his great work.

It is remarked by Brilioth that the rise of the

[1] Yngve Brilioth, *The Anglican Revival*, pp. 1 *seq*. (italics mine).

Puritans as a kind of party of ecclesiastical opposition, at first inside and at a later stage outside the
Church, meant that ' the path of Anglicanism had
already begun to narrow, it no longer had the
confidence of the whole country, when it produced
the work which, on the basis of profound thought,
was to give the classic foundation of this wide vision
of the older Anglicanism.'[1] For Hooker, the national
State and the national Church are identical ; and
yet (as Brilioth remarks) ' Hooker's work marks the
end of the only period in the history of the nation,
when the realisation of this high ideal of a Christian
State, whose other name is the Church, seemed still
possible.   The history of the following centuries
shows us only how gradually it was destroyed.'[2]

The Puritan party, in short, went out, or were
driven out, from the Church.   The flood-tide of the
Reformation, in its Calvinist form, and in other
forms also, had (as Brilioth expresses it) ' seriously
reached England, but now it had to carve out a way
for itself alongside of the main Anglican current.'
When the Restoration, succeeding the temporary
Puritan triumph of the days of the Commonwealth,
' replaced the Episcopal Church in its old home, the
time for a comprehensive policy was past and gone.
The Act of Uniformity became the wall which per-

[1] Brilioth, *op. cit.*, p. 2.   [2] *Ibid.*, p. 3.

manently fenced off the Anglican Church from
natural and fruitful relations with the Reformed
Churches. Its national character gave a wrong idea
of what it was, since it left great hosts of most serious
religious people outside its limits. If by the Test
Act full civic rights were reserved for communicants
at its Altar, this served rather to profane the Sacrament than to extend the principles of the National
Church. Thus the Restoration Church shows us a
narrower Anglicanism than that of Hooker, or even
of Laud. But at the same time, we see more plainly
than before how with the progressive religious
differentiation there emerged from the crucible of
time ' (I am still quoting Brilioth) ' a definite
type of Anglican piety. Its characteristic feature is
humanistic theology, with ever stronger leaning to
the Church of the Greek Fathers, an ascetic ideal of
holiness, which produced types of fine spirituality
akin to the saints of the Middle Ages, and alongside
of it a vein of mystical religion. This direction of
piety, which forms the most definite contribution of
Anglicanism to the gallery of religious types in
Christendom, is of a decidedly Catholic temper. It
can be traced through the century with increasing
plainness, from Andrewes to Ken and Wilson.'[1]

The Church of England of Caroline times stands,

[1] Brilioth, *op. cit.*, pp. 4 *seq.*

then, in a certain sense, in idea and intention for the ideal of a Church at once national and orthodox, though in actual fact it was becoming increasingly clear that the so-called ' national ' Church retained the effective religious allegiance of only a part of the nation, that (despite the widespread vogue of the principle *cuius regio, eius religio*) the divergent religious convictions of Christian minds in a period of controversy were not determined by nationality, and that the Church (despite its establishment) might easily degenerate into an Anglican sect. What was claimed for the Church of England was that she was a Church reformed and yet Catholic ; independent of Rome, and protesting against what were affirmed to be the corruptions and errors of Rome, and yet at the same time neither Lutheran nor Calvinist, but patristic and primitive ; a Church which made its appeal to the Scriptures, and to the light which (as it was believed) might be thrown on their meaning by Christian antiquity and by the writings of early Church Fathers ; a Church which retained the episcopate, which set store by the sacraments, and which carried on into the reformed system (though in a modified form) various traditional practices and rites of the Church which in the Protestant world had been elsewhere abandoned ; a Church orthodox in doctrine, holding fast both to

the Catholic creeds and to the dogmas of the Trinity
and of the Incarnation in their orthodox forms ; a
Church which inclined in certain ways to the theological mind of the Greek and Eastern Church
Fathers, and which, in relation to the particular
controversies most agitated by the warring contemporary Protestant schools of theologians upon
the Continent, was content to pursue, upon the
whole, an indeterminate course, and to make
ambiguous statements.

This last point may be illustrated by reference to
the Thirty-nine Articles. Article XIX (' Of the
Church ') shows the influence of the Lutheran Confession of Augsburg. The infallibility of any particular branch of the Church is by implication denied—
it is asserted, for example, that the Churches of
Jerusalem, Alexandria, Antioch and Rome have all
erred. It is affirmed, however, in Article XX that
' the Church hath power to decree Rites and Ceremonies, and authority in Controversies of Faith.' It
is implied that the ' rites and ceremonies ' decreed
by the Church need not be literally scriptural, or the
affirmations of doctrine couched necessarily in
scriptural terms, but on the other hand that they
must not be contrary to Scripture, and that the
general sense of Scripture is to be followed. The
' Romish doctrine ' on certain specified points is

repudiated, and the scholastic doctrine of Transubstantiation is denied in set terms. It is affirmed, however, that the Body and Blood of Christ is actually ' given, taken, and eaten, in the Supper, only after an heavenly and spiritual manner,' and it is pointed out that ' the mean whereby the Body of Christ is received and eaten in the Supper is Faith.' ' The Wicked, and such as be void of a lively faith ' are not partakers of the spiritual benefit of the sacrament : they rather ' do eat and drink ' . . . ' to their condemnation.' The language used in the Articles with regard to the Eucharist, taken strictly, negates both Transubstantiation on the one hand, and the more minimising Zwinglian interpretation on the other. It is compatible, and was no doubt meant to be compatible, either with the receptionist doctrine of the Calvinists (probably held—though the point is disputed—by Hooker), or with the Lutheran doctrine of Consubstantiation. Still more characteristic of many Anglicans has been the assertion, in some not very clearly defined sense, of a ' spiritual ' doctrine of the Real Presence, combined with a refusal to speculate, or to form a theory of its precise nature.

A distinction is drawn in Article XXV between the ' two Sacraments ordained of Christ our Lord in the Gospel ' and the ' five commonly called Sacraments '. The latter are ' not to be counted for Sacraments of the Gospel ', and are said not to have ' like nature of Sacraments with Baptism and the Lord's Supper ', but to be ' such as have grown partly of the corrupt following of the Apostles, partly are states of life allowed in the Scriptures.' For the use of Unction in any form no provision was made in the Prayer Book, and it was probably intended that this sacrament should be tacitly dropped.[1] Confirmation, Penance, Orders and Matrimony, whether verbally intended still to be called sacraments or not, were in practice retained.

On the subjects of Grace and of Original Sin the Articles are strongly Augustinian—perhaps, as a recent Bampton lecturer in the concluding words of his course has maintained, more deliberately and emphatically so than can really be justified.[2] The Article ' Of Predestination and Election ' is deliberately ambiguous. It affirms that to believe that they are predestined and elected in Christ is ' full of sweet, pleasant, and unspeakable comfort ' to the godly, but that to believe that they are reprobate is exceedingly apt to drive the carnally minded to

[1] Unction of the sick has been revived sporadically in recent times in the Church of England : and the rite of anointing with oil plays a part in the King's Coronation.
[2] N. P. Williams, *The Ideas of the Fall and of Original Sin* (the Bampton Lectures for 1924), pp. 439 *seqq.*

despair. It is best, therefore, to fall back upon what is ' generally set forth to us ' on the subject in Scripture. As a matter of history, both the Arminian and the Calvinist views have been held in the Church of England, and the document known as ' His Majesty's Declaration ', prefixed to the Articles in the time of Archbishop Laud, was intended to check the disputing of divines on this subject.

The Articles, taken as a whole, show the influence, at a number of points, of contemporary controversies, and are, in a general sense, moderately Protestant. But they certainly do not betray the preponderating influence of any one particular school of Reformation theology : they compare favourably in this respect, for example both with the Confession of Augsburg and with the Westminster Confession. They were intended in a number of important ways, to leave room for elasticity, and to be patient of more than one type of interpretation. They exclude, no doubt, both Papists and Puritans ; but they were in a broad sense meant to serve as an official formula of comprehension and of peace.

To affirm, as is sometimes done, that the Church of England combines an official Prayer Book and Ordinal which are in a general sense Catholic with a confession of faith which is Calvinist is not strictly true. Professor Heiler, of Marburg, closely approaches this view when he asserts that the Anglican Church is ' nothing but " a great compromise " between Catholicism and Calvinism ', though he just saves himself from it when he adds that ' an occasional Lutheran intrusion ' serves ' to bring variety to the mixture.'[1] On another page the Professor remarks that ' in the Church of England we come across a Protestant confession of faith which is binding upon all priests and teachers, side by side with a Catholic liturgy from which the faithful may draw nourishment daily for their religious and ecclesiastical life. Yet ' (he adds) ' this confession of faith is not quite Protestant—this liturgy not wholly Catholic.'[2] There is ' a peculiar character of compromise ' in the whole Anglican outlook.[3]

This witness, I would suggest, is essentially true. The Anglican Church—beyond question the most balanced, if the least enthusiastic, of the reformed Churches—whether or not she was deliberately or consciously attempting a synthesis, achieved, in her classical period, what was at best only a compromise. Anything more than this at the time was not possible ; perhaps, in any full sense, it is still not wholly possible even to-day. The Church of England struck out a *via media* in a period of acute religious confusion

---

[1] F. Heiler, ' A Lutheran Review of Anglo-Catholicism,' in the *Church Quarterly Review* for October, 1927, p. 4.
[2] Heiler, *op. cit.*, p. 3.   [3] *Op. cit.*, p. 4.

and conflict, and, in so doing, became inevitably
(like other religious denominations within Christendom) in some sense sectarian. The Anglican and
Episcopalian Church of the period of the great
Caroline divines claimed, indeed, to be Catholic—a
pure and reformed branch of the Church Universal :
but in actual fact it was none the less a particular
sect within Christendom, wholly confined to these
islands, and in outlook (except in the sense that it
appealed, on the basis of scholarship, to the witness
of Christian antiquity) virtually content to be insular.
It was moderate, and it was reasonable, and it was
scholarly. It had produced saints, and it had even
produced martyrs. It was established by law, and
in organisation and scope and theoretical claim it
intended, at least, to be national. But it failed, on
the basis of its particular principles, either to retain
the allegiance of the whole nation, or to make itself
fully understood.

The Church was moderately protestant : the
nation, taken as a whole, was more protestant still.
When toleration was secured, there arose a large
growth of nonconformity, while the Church, on the
other hand, was weakened, and (from the point of
view of any hoped-for future predominance of the
Caroline type of Anglican Churchmanship) perhaps
fatally weakened, by the secession in 1689 of the

Non-jurors. There was a brief flowering period once more of High Churchmanship during the reign of Queen Anne, and there were even the beginnings of a missionary movement—the Society for the Propagation of the Gospel in Foreign Parts was founded in 1701. The death of the Queen in 1714 meant that the Whigs came into power and the Tory and High Church clergy, suspected of Jacobitism, were viewed with suspicion. The Convocations were suppressed, Whigs and Latitudinarians were appointed to Bishoprics, and preferment in the Church became without disguise the reward of political services. The Latitudinarian party, disliking frankly the distinctive doctrines of Anglicanism, conformed (on the basis, no doubt, of a minimising conception of conformity) to the Established Church, on the ground mainly that it happened to be established.

The eighteenth century was the age of reason and common sense. It had its strength, as well as its weakness ; but, viewed in retrospect, its outlook upon life can hardly fail to appear to us now to have been both worldly and shallow ; and this worldliness, beyond question, affected the Church. ' To the Latitudinarians ' (remarks Wakeman), ' Protestant mysticism '—Wakeman has here in mind more particularly the Baptists and Quakers—' was as hateful as High Church sacerdotalism. They sought to overcome both by insisting on the supremacy of reason in faith as well as practice, and denouncing enthusiasm.'[1]

We are sometimes warned not to depreciate eighteenth-century England unduly, and there was at least a real intellectual life, and some genuine piety, within the Church, even in the age of the Deists. Dr. Brilioth reminds us that 'it was the controversy between Deism and Orthodoxy which produced the most important work of theological and religious literature in the century, alongside of Law's *Serious Call*, Bishop Butler's *Analogy* (1736).'[2] But the prefatory *Advertisement* prefixed to the *Analogy*, even if allowance be made for a certain amount of quiet irony on the part of the writer, itself goes far to bear out the prevailing impression of the period, and to justify Brilioth's description of it elsewhere as ' the golden age of practical materialism '.[3] ' It is come, I know not how,' writes Bishop Butler, ' to be taken for granted, by many persons, that Christianity is not so much as a subject of inquiry : but that it is, now at length, discovered to be fictitious. And accordingly they treat it, as if, in the present age, this were an agreed point among all people of

[1] Wakeman, *op. cit.*, p. 410.
[2] Brilioth, *op. cit.*, p. 21.
[3] Brilioth, *op. cit.*, p. 9.

discernment, and nothing remained, but to set it up as a principal subject of mirth and ridicule, as it were by way of reprisals, for its having so long interrupted the pleasures of the world.'[1]

Evidence, such as Butler supplies, of the prevailing tone of polite society is indeed no necessary index of the actual state of religious life in the Church as a whole ; but it is certain that, here too, there were many abuses, much laxity, and a general atmosphere of neglect and indifference. Descriptions are frequent in literature of the type of the Squarson, ' a compound of squire and parson, who lived his comfortable life as an honest landed proprietor, took a lively part in the neighbourhood's more or less robust pleasures, hunted, ate and drank,' and was ' at the best the worldly-wise indispensable adviser of his flock ', to whom ' Sunday came as a slight interruption in the agreeable round ' of his days, and who ' certainly . . . was not guilty of the error of appealing to the emotional possibilities, which perhaps still lurked in his hearers, by any care whatever for the outward forms of divine service.'[2] Even the late Professor H. M. Gwatkin, than whom it would be difficult to find a writer more robustly Erastian and Protestant, was constrained to end his book, *Church and State in England to the Death of*

---

[1] Bishop Butler, *Analogy* (Gladstone's Edn., pp. 1 *seq*).
[2] Brilioth, *op. cit.*, pp. 8 *seq*.

Queen Anne, with the remark that ' the age of Walpole was an age of stagnation.'[1] Mr. Gladstone, in *Gleanings of Past Years*, puts the case, as regards the condition of the English Church even so late as the beginning of the nineteenth century, with cold trenchancy :

' For many years ' (he writes), ' perhaps for some generations, Christendom might have been challenged to show, either then or from any former age, a clergy (with exceptions) so secular and lax, or congregations so cold, irreverent and indevout.'

And again (in a later essay contained in the same collection) :

' Our services were probably without a parallel in the world for their debasement. As they would have shocked a Brahmin or a Buddhist, so they could hardly have been endured in this country had not the faculty of taste, and the perception of the seemly or unseemly, been as dead as the spirit of devotion.'[2]

It is not difficult to understand that there were some who regarded the Church in this period as being little more than a department of State. The demonstration of the fact that the Church was indeed more than this is to be sought and found in the story of the Evangelical and Tractarian revivals.

[1] Gwatkin, *op. cit.*, p. 392.
[2] W. E. Gladstone, *op. cit.*, Vol. VII, p. 137 ; Vol. VI, p. 119 (quoted by Heiler in *C.Q.R.*, Vol. CV, p. 9).

E

CHAPTER III

MOVEMENTS AND TENDENCIES WITHIN THE CHURCH

IN the year 1729 John Wesley and his friends formed in Oxford what came to be known as the ' Holy Club ', for the deepening of their own spiritual lives. A strict Churchman, Wesley inculcated upon his followers, and practised himself, the rigid observance of the festivals and fasts of the Church, diligence in prayer and in the examination of conscience, almsgiving, deeds of charity, and weekly communion. The life of Wesley is not here and now to be written. He remained to the end of his days a strict Churchman. A time came when, despairing of the inertia and lack of sympathy displayed by the authorities of the Church, he traversed Church order. In 1784, having persuaded himself that the presbyterate was endowed with the same powers as the episcopate, he consecrated two ' superintendents ' for the Methodists of America, thereby paving the way for the inevitable breach. Nevertheless, it was not by Wesley's own wish or desire—it was rather against his injunctions—that the Methodists seceded, and severed themselves from the Church of England.

The Evangelical Revival was in its essence a revival of spiritual and personal religion in an age of spiritual torpor. It was a new and fervent proclamation of the Church's primary Gospel—the Gospel of divine love, grace and power, of forgiveness of sinners, and of salvation from sin. At the same time, despite Wesley's own Churchmanship, its sources of inspiration were not purely Anglican. There was a renewed contact with the Evangelical religion and theology of the Continent. John Wesley himself had been in close personal relations with representatives of the Moravian Brethren, a pietistic Lutheran sect, and both John and Charles Wesley had read Luther's commentaries on the Epistles to the Galatians and Romans. It was on May 24, 1738, that John Wesley ' felt his heart strangely warmed ' at the meeting in Aldersgate Street, when he ' felt he did trust in Christ, Christ alone, for salvation ' ; ' and ' (he adds) ' an assurance was given me that He had taken away *my* sins, even *mine*, and saved *me* from the law of sin and death.' His brother Charles had experienced a day or two earlier a similar ' conversion '. What the experience meant to them both is expressed in the rapturous ecstasy of Charles Wesley's hymns.

The preaching of the two brothers Wesley, of George Whitefield, and of others who sympathised with them, went like wildfire throughout England, evoking a new and exultant tide of revived spiritual life.   With the secession of the Wesleyan societies proper from the Church, and with the theological breach between Wesley and Whitefield on the question of predestination, we are not now primarily concerned.   Our concern is with the Evangelical Movement within Anglicanism.   It has, however, been pointed out (and it is a thing strangely para-doxical) that, with the exception of those Calvinistic Methodists who followed Whitefield and Lady Huntingdon, it was precisely the *Arminian* section of Methodism which forsook the communion of the parent Church and went out into the wilderness. Wesley himself and his brother Charles and their followers believed firmly in the universality of the love of God, and of the hymns of Charles Wesley a considerable number are directed controversially against the ' horrible decrees ' of the Calvinists. Men like Hervey, Grimshaw, Berridge, Romaine, and the rest, who remained within the Church of England, were, on the other hand, doctrinally Calvinists :   and the Church of England is not a Calvinist body.   The leaders of the Tractarian Move-ment of later days, in so far as they reacted against the Evangelicalism in which not a few of them had been brought up, were reacting primarily against Calvinism.

The Calvinism, however, of the great Evangelicals was perhaps (as it has been suggested) in certain respects a mitigated Calvinism. The Evangelicals were not primarily theologians—it may be said, perhaps, generally that the Evangelicals within the Church of England have never been great as theological thinkers. Despite the fact that they based their conception of religion upon the total depravity of human nature, they employed this conception (as Wakeman remarks) rather ' to magnify the love of God in redemption ' than ' to prove His justice in condemnation '.[1]   It is, moreover, probable that other than Calvinist influences also came in.   ' Evangelicalism within the Church ', remarks Brilioth, ' was certainly not altogether withdrawn from Lutheran influence, which in time made itself more strongly felt.'[2]

Evangelicalism, in effect, stood primarily for the conscious acceptance of Christ as a personal Saviour and Deliverer from sin's guilt and power.   That was the heart and core of its message, to which theological theory was in a certain sense secondary.   Doubtless

[1] Wakeman, *op. cit.*, p. 450.
[2] Brilioth, *op. cit.*, p. 31.

a new doctrinal orientation was involved, in which the dogmas of Sin, of Atonement, and of Sanctification displaced Christology and the Incarnation from the centre of theological interest.   But it might be claimed that the Evangelicals were here redressing a balance ; and if they proclaimed also the Lutheran doctrine of ' assurance ', the general need for explicit ' conversion ', justification by faith only, and the utterly lost state of mankind apart from conscious relation to Christ, it might be urged that—in terms of the thought of their age and in relation to their own unmistakable spiritual experience—they were proclaiming the central Gospel of Christianity with power.   They were Puritan, rigid, and intellectually narrow ; but they were holy men of God, filled with burning enthusiasm and with zeal for the conversion of sinners.   They were the protagonists in missionary enterprise and in philanthropic activity.   Despite all their defects and limitations—and it has become the fashion in modern times to dwell upon these—they have profoundly influenced the inner life of the Church of England for good.

The Evangelicals who remained within the Church claimed to be loyal to Anglicanism—sometimes, indeed (more especially in later times, and in opposition to Anglo-Catholicism), going so far as to maintain that their own particular version of

Anglicanism was the only legitimate one. Judged, as a matter of fact, by historical standards, their position, however legitimate, was not in a typical sense Anglican. They conformed, indeed, to the Church : they had every right to belong to her, and they have vindicated that right by their subsequent history, by the work that they have done, and by the service which they have rendered. But that does not make them strict Anglicans, in the historical sense of that word. They have been no more strictly Anglican than the Anglo-Catholics, and much less so than the Tractarians.

Accepting and valuing the Episcopate, not as a matter of principle, but as a convenient form of Church government, the Evangelicals within the Church have traditionally set store by the Establishment. At one time fiercely opposed, upon grounds mainly political and social, to Nonconformity, they have in more recent days tended rather (reversing this attitude) to co-operate on friendly terms with Dissent, and to look towards union. They have accepted the Thirty-nine Articles, placing upon them the more avowedly Protestant of the two or more variant interpretations which that ambiguous theological instrument is capable of bearing. The Prayer Book they have both accepted and valued, though without (as a rule) carrying out its directions in full :

and there have been parts of the Prayer Book system about which they have never been comfortable— they have, in fact, tended in relation to the Prayer Book (like other classes of Churchmen) to use and appreciate such parts of the Book as appealed to them, and to ignore as obsolete such parts as did not. Conversely (again like other bodies of Churchmen), they have supplemented in various ways the provision made in the Prayer Book for worship— more especially by the adoption of Prayer Meetings, and by the introduction of hymns.

' During the latter part of the eighteenth century ', writes Wakeman, ' the Evangelical party were the salt of the Church of England. The connection of their earlier leaders, such as Hervey and Romaine, with Whitefield no doubt stamped them as fanatics in the eyes of educated men, and made them intensely unpopular. As with the Tractarians of the next century, it was a very long time before the gates of palaces and deaneries were thrown open to them. But the years of unpopularity were by no means years of loss. They won their way gradually to importance by the sheer force of piety and character.'[1] A time came when they were, to all intents and purposes, the predominant party in the Church. During the first half of the nineteenth century (I

[1] Wakeman, *op. cit.*, pp. 452 *seq.*

again quote Wakeman) ' the most influential and the most popular of the clergy were permeated ' by the spirit of Evangelicalism, ' even if they did not definitely range themselves under its banners. To be religious meant in the language of the day, as the novels show us, to forswear dancing and the theatre, to keep Sunday strictly, to " sit under " a popular preacher on Sundays, to be sober in dress and staid in manner, to supplement the Bible with Venn's *Complete Duty of Man*, or Wilberforce's *Practical View*, and to be interested in foreign missions.

' But ' (the historian adds), ' no sooner had Evangelicalism become popular than it ceased to produce great men. It is astonishing how few men of mark adorned the episcopate from the beginning of the century until the consecration of Samuel Wilberforce in 1845. It is sad to find how few abuses in the Church were remedied, until the energy of the Parliament of 1832 forced the question to the front, and dealt with it trenchantly if not always wisely. . . . Individuals such as Charles Simeon exercised a magnetic influence upon those with whom they were brought into contact, but except as individuals they never attempted to grapple with the terrible problems occasioned by the enormous increase of population and the growth of industrial towns. . . . Their best men devoted themselves to mission work, like John Venn, or set up proprietary chapels in fashionable watering-places. . . . They failed to lead the Church just when it most needed leadership.'[1]

Wakeman's history is written, no doubt, with a purpose ; and its purpose is not primarily to glorify the Evangelical party. The remarks just quoted, nevertheless, do not appear to be substantially unfair. The neo-Evangelicalism of our own time, as expressed, for example, through the ' Evangelical Group Movement ', is more difficult to estimate. It is certainly not lacking in social enthusiasm ; it is fully alive to the ' terrible problems ' ; and it is eager to be in touch with modernity. It has lost much of the narrowness of the old Evangelicalism. It is unhappily not clear that it may not, in the process of becoming liberalised, be in some danger at times of losing its sureness of hold upon the central message of the Evangelical Gospel. Evangelicalism has beyond question been harder hit by New Testament criticism than any other tradition or ' school of thought ' within the Church, precisely for the reason that its earlier intellectual foundations were regarded as being in the strictest and narrowest sense Biblical. The more constructive post-critical Evangelical theology of modern Germany is not easily popularised, and has as yet hardly begun to

[1] Wakeman, *op. cit.*, p. 455.

exert any very appreciable influence in England. Further consideration of the position as it exists to-day must be postponed to the last lecture. I proceed now to invite your attention to the second of the two great modern religious movements which came out of Oxford—that which we know as Tractarianism.

Professor Brilioth has argued (rightly, I think) that there was a real connexion between the two movements. The Tractarians, as he points out, were in great measure recruited from Evangelicals ; and of those in particular who went over to Rome, not a few, before marching from Oxford to Rome, had marched already from Clapham to Oxford.[1] Mr. Gladstone is quoted as having remarked that ' the Evangelical movement filled men so full with the wine of spiritual life that larger and better vessels were required to hold it.'[2] I myself well remember a distinguished and still living Anglo-Catholic once saying to me that he had begun life as an Evangelical, and that he claimed to be an Evangelical still : he had been brought to believe in an objective Gift or Real Presence of Christ in the Eucharist, independent of any particular merit or faith on the part of the individual recipient, partly at least on the ground

[1] Brilioth, *op. cit.*, p. 43.
[2] Brilioth, *loc. cit.*

that only so (as he held) could he retain his right to sing the familiar lines of the Evangelical hymn :

> ' Nothing in my hand I bring ;
> Simply to Thy Cross I cling.'

The Tractarian or Anglo-Catholic type of churchmanship has been at its best, and has exhibited its greatest power of appeal, when it has been combined (as it was combined, for example, in the persons of such men as the late Father Dolling or the late Father Stanton) with a real Evangelicalism. The two movements, rightly considered, are complementary ; and the Tractarians, or many of them, owed a debt to the Evangelical movement of which (divided as they came to be from the Evangelicals alike in theology and in religious and ecclesiastical practice) they were not always explicitly conscious.

Tractarianism, properly so called, is by common consent held to date from Keble's famous Assize Sermon on National Apostasy in 1832. The movement, in other words, began with the sounding of a note of alarm, provoked by what were considered to be the dangerously Erastian and liberalising tendencies of the age. The neo-Anglicanism of the Tractarians was thus in a certain sense a reactionary movement. It looked backwards towards the past. From one point of view, it was an attempt to go

behind the whole Hanoverian period, and, in an age
of neglect and of apparently growing indifference, to
revive the strict churchmanship of Caroline times.
Its leaders pressed the appeal of the Anglican Church
to the Scriptures, but to the Scriptures as interpreted by early tradition. As against the prevalent
' liberalism ', they rested on authority—a religion of
revelation, they believed, must be a religion of
authority ; and they found their authority, not
simply in the Anglican tradition (though they
appealed, of course, to the great seventeenth-century
Anglicans), but in the voice (as they conceived it)
of the undivided Church of patristic days. The
consentient mind of the Church of the Fathers and
of the Ecumenical Councils they believed to be
infallible. Here was the true teaching Church, which
could make its appeal to the Scriptures, and which
could find there the evidences or ' proof ' of its
teaching. After the great division between the
Church of the East and the Church of the West there
had ensued many corruptions—more especially in
the West, where the Church of Rome had been the
great innovator, and the great corrupter of the truth.
The Tractarians were strongly anti-Roman, and
their view of Church history was romantic. The
Church of England (they believed) at the time of
the Reformation had rejected the corruptions of

Rome, but had preserved all that was really Catholic
—that which had been believed and practised everywhere, and at all times, and by all Christians,
wherever the true Apostolical succession had been
preserved. Catholic truth might in fact be defined
as that view of Christianity in which Constantinople,
Rome, and Canterbury agreed.

The Church of England had faults—there was very
much in her present condition which was unsatisfactory, and a considerable proportion of her actual
members were blind to her real nature. There were
those who confused her with a Protestant sect : but
she was not really this, inasmuch as she had preserved, by a true succession, the Catholic Episcopate,
the Catholic Creeds, and the Catholic Sacraments.
The real truth about the Church of England, the
Tractarians maintained, was the truth as the Tractarians conceived it. Underlying their position, in
the form in which they themselves held it, was the
' three-branch ' theory of the Church, the belief in
ecclesiastical infallibility, and the crucial importance
which they attached to the doctrine and fact of
Apostolical Succession.

Starting from these fundamental convictions as a
basis, they set themselves to recall men to a renewed
appreciation of the forgotten treasures of the Church,
to the wealth of the spiritual riches involved in the

inheritance which had come down to her of liturgy, rite, and sacramental tradition and practice—and to a remarkable extent they succeeded. The precise intellectual position of the Tractarians is defended to-day by no serious theological thinker—certainly not by the more intelligent of those who in our own time would be called Anglo-Catholics. Nevertheless, the results of the movement are everywhere.

'The Oxford Movement . . .', writes the Bishop of Gloucester, ' was undoubtedly the greatest movement of religious thought of the nineteenth century, not only in England but elsewhere ; and its influence has been by no means limited to this country, nor has it yet ceased. It might almost be said that there are many countries which are now just beginning to feel the effects of its influence. . . . The first point about the Oxford Movement was that in a world which was largely not religious at all, but if it was religious cared little for the external form of religion, it boldly asserted the voice of the Church, the religion of Sacraments, external worship, organisation, and all those embodiments of the religious spirit which people had begun to look upon almost with contempt. . . . The Church gradually learnt the value of external aids to religion, beauty of worship, music, after a little time ritual and ceremonial, architecture, painting. All was assimilated by this new movement

of thought, which for England, and many countries
outside England, has done much to transform the
religious life. . . .

' What were the permanent contributions of the
Movement to religious thought ?   I think that the
most widespread has been the revival of the idea of
the Church.   How widespread that is, may be seen
at the present day by the desire for Christian reunion
through all the religious bodies, and in almost every
country.   The Lutheran, the Presbyterian, the
Wesleyan are asserting at the present day all the
ecclesiastical side of their tradition in a way which
their grandfathers could not have understood.   The
individualism in religion which made any corporate
reunion appear quite unnecessary has everywhere
passed away, and although we may find it difficult
to agree upon the definition of a Church, or to find
a means of uniting the scattered elements of Christianity, yet it is because of the new impetus to
corporate Christianity which the Oxford Movement
first started that we are all at any rate desiring to
do this.'[1]

Of the two movements thus far considered I have
myself elsewhere written some words which (with
slight modifications) I here venture to quote.

' Both Movements have in a sense found inherited

---

[1] Bishop of Gloucester, Preface to Brilioth, *op. cit.*, pp. vi-ix.

Anglicanism too narrow for them. The Evangelical
Movement, in so far as it has remained within the
parent Church, has conformed to Anglicanism as
interpreted in the Evangelical sense. . . But it has
looked beyond the borders of Anglicanism to Evangelical Christianity at large, is at the present time
anxious for reunion with English Nonconformity and
with Protestant Christianity in general, and has
borrowed religious usages and modes of worship
supplementary to the Prayer Book from Protestant
sources. The Oxford Movement, originally simply a
High Church Movement, meticulously Anglican,
careful of precedent, archæological in outlook, seek-
ing its inspiration in the past, and appealing to the
New Testament and to the Fathers of the first six
centuries of Christianity, when it moved out into the
parishes and gave its strength to the work of reviving
and building up Church life, especially in the slums
of the great cities, became more romantic and
adventurous. It revived ceremonial. It revived the
religious life, both for men and for women. It
ceased to be limited by the first six centuries, and
like the Evangelical Movement it has looked beyond
Anglicanism. It has borrowed religious usages and
modes of worship from Catholic Christianity in
general, and more immediately from Rome. Necessarily it rejects the distinctively Roman position and

F

the claims of the Papacy, but it has to a large extent lost its original anti-Romanism. It is anxious for reunion with Catholic Christianity generally—that is to say, with Rome and with the East.'[1]

The prospects of such reunion, more especially in relation to Rome, are indeed not immediately hopeful. It was right that the recent Conversations between Roman Catholic and Anglican divines, held at Malines under the chairmanship of the late Cardinal Mercier between the years 1921 and 1925,[2] should take place. It was intelligible that the Anglican representatives—more especially in view of the fact that the Conference (though in its later stages it had the cognizance both of the Archbishops of Canterbury and York and of the Holy See) was to a large extent unofficial—should have been chosen from among those who might be counted upon to be antecedently not unsympathetic towards the idea of reunion in this particular direction. That the results, despite some measure of mutual clarification of mind, should have been disappointing and meagre, was only what was to be expected. The cleavage of mind between Roman and Anglican would indeed have appeared more far-reaching and more fundamental if repre-

[1] A. E. J. Rawlinson, *Authority and Freedom*, pp. 171 *seq.*, adapted and slightly abridged.
[2] *The Conversations at Malines*, 1921–25 (Oxford University Press, 1927).

sentatives of the younger intellectuals of modern
Anglo-Catholicism had taken part in the conference,
and had frankly declared their whole mind.   The
official mentality of Rome is not that of the modern
world, and the Church of Rome is not ripe for
reunion upon any terms which would not involve the
acceptance of its own traditional and unmodified
claims.   The problem of Christian reunion must
moreover in any case be envisaged in terms not of
Catholicism only (in the narrower sense of that word),
but of Christendom as a whole.   Rome and the East
have indeed contributions to make of a vital kind to
the reunited Church of the ultimate future—contributions determined in each case by the elements of
real value and truth in the specific genius of their
respective religious traditions.   But no reunion in
either of these directions is possible until both
Orthodoxy and Rome have proceeded a great deal
farther than either of them has so far succeeded in
doing towards an appreciation, not indeed of the
mere negations of Protestantism, but of the real and
positive contribution which Protestant theology has,
in its own way, been enabled to make to the fuller
religious understanding of the Gospel, as well as of
the positive meaning and value of religious and
ecclesiastical freedom.

Religious, intellectual, and ecclesiastical freedom—

the demonstration that these things are possible, and that they are possible, upon a basis of more or less ordered liberty, within the framework and fellowship of a single religious denomination or ' Church ',[1] has been the result, in quite recent times, of the clash and relative tension between the two main versions of Anglicanism, fertilised (both of them) by mutual criticism, and by the contribution (and it has been a very important contribution) of the third great movement or tendency within the Church of England, the so-called ' Broad Church ' or intellectual movement.

The Broad Church movement of Victorian times may be said to go back to the group known as the Noetics, the contemporaries of Newman at Oriel College, Oxford ; or again (though the succession here is less close) to an earlier group at the sister University, the so-called Cambridge Platonists of the mid-seventeenth century. The work of Coleridge, who, as a lay theologian, was in contact with German idealist thought, and who (as Canon Storr has remarked) ' was the intellectual father of the philosophical movement which was continued by Julius Hare and Maurice.'[2] was for the earlier part of the

[1] By the term ' Church ' in this connection I mean an authentic manifestation of Christendom which claims for itself Catholicity, and which aspires to be more than a sect.

[2] V. F. Storr, *Development of English Theology in the Nineteenth Century*, p. 317.

nineteenth century of special importance. Maurice, F. W. Robertson, Kingsley, Thomas Arnold, Stanley, Thirlwall, and Milman, and a generation or so later Hatch, Hort, Creighton, Westcott, Lightfoot, Driver, Sanday—these are great names, the owners of which have, in various ways, profoundly influenced the whole intellectual outlook of modern Anglican Christianity. It would not be possible to classify any of them as having belonged definitely to the Evangelical, still less to the Tractarian, tradition : but it has been chiefly thanks to their work, and to the work of others like them, that the Church of England in modern times has been enabled to keep closely in touch with contemporary philosophical thought and speculation upon the one hand, and with the methods and results of historical criticism and of modern scientific research on the other.

The work of such men as those I have named has borne fruit, and has exercised influence, outside the Church of England no less than within it ; and it has itself been fostered by influences coming from without, and more especially from Germany. The work of scholarship is international, and its results are the perquisite of no particular Church, and still less of any particular ecclesiastical party. The special controversies which agitated the ecclesiastical world in Victorian times in relation to those who were accounted Broad Churchmen—' the *Essays and Reviews* debate ', the unorthodoxy of Bishop Colenso, the strange and unedifying opposition which was offered, on the ground of his theological opinions, to the proposal that Jowett should be paid an adequate stipend as Professor of Greek, and the attempts to prosecute him for heresy—all these things would to-day be regarded, presumably, by Churchmen of virtually all schools of thought as being only the echo of

> ' faint, unhappy, far-off things
> And battles long ago.'

The spirit of heresy-hunting still from time to time, no doubt, raises its head, but no longer with very much chance of success.   Broadly speaking, the battle of intellectual liberty within the Church of England has been decisively fought and decisively won : and the results of that victory have become part of the common heritage, in greater or less degree, of the intellectual leaders (and of the rank and file also, in so far as they choose, or care, to be intellectually free) of all schools of theological and ecclesiastical thought.

The intellectual revolution which has taken place within (shall we say ?) the period of the last fifty or sixty years is enormous.   It has affected not so much the conclusions of theological thought—though there are, no doubt, many important respects and particulars in which they, too, have not been left unaffected—as its methods. The whole mode of approach to theological questions, wherever what may be broadly described as the modern spirit has penetrated (and it has penetrated very widely), has been given a new orientation. The theologian of to-day, of whatever ecclesiastical affiliation or party, is aware, more or less consciously, that he breathes a new atmosphere, and that he is in contact with a new temper of mind. Many of the old controversies have become virtually obsolete ; and even in cases in which this is not so, the issues present themselves to-day in new forms, and must be approached under largely new categories of thought, and considered afresh in the light of new knowledge—philosophical, scientific, or historical, as the case may demand. The old faith, we are commonly told, needs re-statement. Those who are often called ' modernists ' (of all schools of thought) have essayed the task of re-statement. Even when the results have been unsatisfactory or needlessly disturbing, the wisest among those who have criticised them have made it the ground of their complaint, not that the attempt has been made to re-state Christianity, but that the resulting statement has not been fully Christian. A living and robust faith (it is now widely recognised),

if it is to enter adequately into its intellectual
heritage, and to proclaim the Gospel with efficacy
and power to the living minds of to-day, requires an
environment of intellectual and spiritual freedom
as the very atmosphere in which it must breathe.
To have vindicated this claim within the Church, and
to have vindicated it effectively, has been the great
service which was rendered by those who in the days
of the late Queen Victoria were known as ' Broad
Churchmen ' ; and their victory was sealed by an
alteration in the formula of subscription to the
Articles.

Previously to the year 1865, an Anglican candidate
for Holy Orders was required to sign his name to a
statement as follows : ' I, A.B., do willingly and
from my heart subscribe to the Thirty-nine Articles
of Religion and to the three articles in the Thirty-
sixth Canon, and to all things therein contained.'
When Newman and his friends, at the beginning of
the Tractarian Movement, propounded their catholic-
izing interpretation of Anglicanism, the question was
everywhere asked, ' What do these men make of the
Articles ? '   The reply was Tract XC, in which
Newman showed, though (as his opponents complained) by the use of a certain amount of perhaps
over-ingenious pleading, that the Articles (in certain
particulars, as I have already suggested, ambiguous)

might, on the whole, be interpreted in a virtually
Catholic sense.   Whatever might or might not be
thought of the morality of Newman's Tract XC,
the Broad Churchmen, no less than the Tractarians,
were in certain respects galled by the Articles ; and
(unlike the Tractarians) they had influence in high
places, and were in a position to bring it about that
the formula of subscription was altered.   The
authorities of Church and State, advised by a Royal
Commission, recognised at length that the difficulties
created by the old form of subscription were real.
Doctrinal uniformity within the Church could not in
fact be secured by such means, and the consciences
of many of the clergy were strained.   Specific subscription in the old form to the Thirty-nine Articles
was accordingly by the concurrent action of the
Convocations and of Parliament abolished, and by
the Clerical Subscription Act of 1865 there was
substituted the present requirement of an ' assent ',
given in quite general terms, to the Articles, Prayer
Book, and Ordinal, taken together.

The clergy, therefore, no longer in the strict sense
' subscribe ' to the Articles.   What they actually do
is to affirm generally that the ' doctrine of the Church
of England ', as ' set forth ' in the Articles, Prayer
Book, and Ordinal, is ' agreeable to the Word of
God ' ;   and they undertake, further, in public

prayer and administration of the Sacraments, to use the form prescribed in the Prayer Book ' and none other, except so far as shall be ordered by lawful authority '. Casuistical questions no doubt remain as to what precisely may be regarded as being covered by the phrase ' lawful authority '. The Prayer Book in current practice is not as a rule followed with absolute strictness : and the promise to use its forms, like all formulæ of ' assent ' in a living Church, must be held to be governed and interpreted, for practical purposes, by the actual practice and present mind of the religious communion in which ' assent ' or subscription takes place. Broadly it may be said that the Prayer Book of 1662, supplemented, so far as may be needful, by the ' additions and deviations ' contained in the revised Book ' as proposed in 1928 ' (which have moral, though not in the strict sense legal, authority), serves the Church still as a general standard or norm in public worship ; and that the Articles, Prayer Book, and Ordinal, taken together, serve as an historical standard or norm as regards Anglican doctrine.

It was the manifest intention of the change which was made by the Act of 1865 to relax stringency of subscription. The declaration of Assent, in its present form, cannot, in view of this fact, be held reasonably to commit those who make it to anything more than a generally Anglican position. It is a formula of general, and not of detailed, ' assent ' ; and it is not in present practice interpreted to mean more than this fact would imply. The altered form of Assent (the significance of which, despite the fact that it has been in operation for two generations, has hardly been grasped by the public at large) has in effect operated as a charter of very genuine intellectual liberty and (within limits) also of practical liberty, to the clergy of all schools of thought.[1]

The Evangelical, the Tractarian, and the Liberal or ' Broad Church ' Movements of thought and of life within the Church of England, as they existed and perhaps to a certain extent mutually strove with one another in the Church of the last century, have now been briefly surveyed. The survey will have wholly failed of its purpose if the effect has not been to provoke once more the familiar reflection that the Church has owed much to all three ; but to suggest perhaps also the thought that an end might reasonably be found for some at least of these controversies, and that a more synthetic interpretation, not merely of Anglicanism, but of the meaning of Christianity

[1] The XXXIX Articles do not in any case or in any sense bind the laity of the Church of England, unless the 5th Canon of 1604, which enjoins that the laity shall not attack them, be regarded as still having force.

as a whole, may in the providence of God be beginning to emerge.

It will be the concern of the last lecture to attempt an estimate of the condition of the Church of England to-day, and of the prospects of hope for the future. Only in the context of such an attempt may it be possible to attempt also to find or to indicate some kind of an answer to the question with which these lectures began.

CHAPTER IV

THE ANGLICAN CHURCH AND THE FUTURE

THE Anglican Church is no longer specifically English. The Church in England itself, indeed, retains still, even under modern conditions, close national associations and national ties. Its history has been intimately intertwined with the history and life of the people of England for a period of considerably more than a thousand years, and it has ever regarded itself as being commissioned to proclaim the Gospel and to administer the sacraments of Christ to all such members of the nation as were prepared to accept its message and to conform to its spiritual discipline. In the two provinces, moreover, of Canterbury and York—though in those two provinces only—the Church still stands to the State in the legal relationship commonly described as ' Establishment '.

The relations between Church and State which fall under this head are at the present time notoriously unsatisfactory. The instructive introduction prefixed by the Bishop of Durham to his recently-published charge on the subject of *Disestablishment*

may be read with advantage even by those who do
not share necessarily in detail all the particular
convictions of the Bishop with regard to ecclesiastical
matters.   The possibilities of friction between Church
and State under modern conditions are of more than
one kind.   They may affect doctrine, worship and
spiritual discipline.   They may affect also morals,
more especially in respect of such questions as are
concerned with the ethics of marriage and divorce.
' The Morality of Christ ', writes the Bishop of
Durham, is to-day ' heavily challenged throughout
Christendom, and in some important departments
(e.g., marriage) has been openly repudiated.   In
these circumstances the ancient intimacy of Church
and State has created a formidable danger by pre-
disposing the unreflecting multitude to assume that
what the State enacts must necessarily accord with
what the Church teaches.   The ordinary Englishman
is not accustomed to distinguish between a Moral
Law, Divine in origin, authority, and sanction, which
the Church has received from the Hands of Christ,
and must at all costs maintain, and the current
morality of English Society, which may or may not
accord with the Christian Law, and which alone
determines the legislation of the State and the " use
and wont " of popular life.'[1]

[1] Bishop of Durham, *op. cit.*, **pp.** 81 *seq.*

In the sphere of doctrine, worship and spiritual discipline the clash between Church and State has within the last few months become open and manifest. The strict letter of the existing law in these matters has for generations been widely ignored, and is in practice unworkable. The attempt of the Church, under the provisions of the Enabling Act, to secure its amendment in due constitutional form has been twice rejected by Parliament. The Enabling Act, which by its promoters had been designed with the idea of securing at least relative and practical freedom for the Church, has manifestly failed of its purpose. Regard for historical and constitutional precedent had dictated the retention, under the Act, of an ultimate parliamentary veto in respect of ecclesiastical measures ; and the House of Commons, stirred by the eloquence of a passionate minority, availed itself of its strict legal rights even in a matter which concerned purely worship and discipline. The late Archbishop of Canterbury, addressing the National Assembly on July 2, 1928, affirmed that the Church must ' retain its inalienable right to formulate its faith and to arrange its forms of worship.' ' No one ', he said, ' can challenge that principle as a principle.' Despite the Archbishop's words, the majority of the speeches made in the House of Commons, as well as the votes which were

given, were a direct challenge to the Archbishop's
' principle ', and the whole tenour of the debate was,
no less than its result, an assertion of the most naked
and unabashed form of Erastianism.

That the Bishops, clergy, and worshipping laity of
the Church of England have been involved in a
situation which the Bishop of Durham describes as
' cruel and humiliating ', and the Archbishop of York
as being ' in the strict and proper sense of the word
intolerable ', is obvious.   In the exercise of what is
described as their ' inherent administrative discretion ', the Archbishops and Bishops, in the
majority of dioceses, and with the approval in general
terms of their policy by the Lower Houses of Convocation in the two Provinces,[1] have announced
their intention henceforward, in all cases in which
such departure is seriously desired by the clergy and
worshipping people, of treating the standards and
forms of the defeated Prayer Book of 1928 as the
norm of informally tolerated departure from the
standards of 1662.   They have denied that in so
doing they are, in strictness, ' flouting ' the judgment
of Parliament.   Their position rests upon the fact
that the authority of the revised Book is not legal,
but moral.   From the point of view of strict law, to
use the new Prayer Book is not more illegal than to

[1] See Appendix I, pp. 161 *seqq*.

fail to use strictly the old one ; and it would be absurd (as the Archbishop of York has remarked) to suggest that, among currently-practised departures from the letter of an obsolete law, those alone are to be reprobated which have been deliberately approved by the authorities of the Church. At the same time, there is an obvious sense in which the declared policy of the Episcopate does, in substance, amount to a virtual ' flouting ' of Parliament ; and it would have been well to acknowledge frankly this fact.

Nevertheless, that the Episcopate of the Church is, at the present time, morally and spiritually bound to refuse absolutely to accept the implied claim of the House of Commons to be the arbiter, under modern conditions, of the Church's system of worship, I for one cannot doubt. A distinguished Lutheran divine said to me, not long ago, that in his judgment the Anglican Bishops were bound at this juncture to stand up to the State : to accept the verdict of Parliament would be (he said) in effect to acquiesce in the attempt to assert a form of Erastianism which, if it were asserted successfully, would go far to deprive the Church of England of its right to be considered a true and spiritually ' valid ' branch of the Church Catholic. Disestablishment, as the Bishop of Durham and others point out, may be the logical sequel : and Disestablishment may become, sooner

G

or later, inevitable. The alternative would be some
form of readjustment, some revision or modification
of the present relation of the Church to the State,
upon lines more religiously and spiritually tolerable.
' The poison of " Erastianism ",' remarks the Bishop
of Durham, ' has penetrated deeply, and the
" Erastian " habit of thought and speech has
carried some Anglican divines to strange lengths.'[1]
It is the growing conviction, nevertheless, of perhaps
the majority of actively practising Churchmen, of
more than one ' school of thought ', that at least the
present form of Establishment must in the relatively
near future be either mended or ended.

Opposition to the suggestion that full liberty of
self-government in respect of doctrinal, liturgical and
spiritual matters might with advantage be conceded
to the Anglican Church in the two provinces of its
communion which are at present ' established ' rests,
in the quarters in which such opposition is deserving
of respect, on the fear (based presumably on the
experience of Victorian times) that the Church might
make itself narrow—that it might, in effect, turn
itself into a defined and rigidly-disciplined sect. It
is sometimes pointed out that the Gorham judgment,
in the year 1850, and the Bennett judgment, in 1871,[2]

[1] Bishop of Durham, *op. cit.*, p. 82.
[2] In the Gorham case the Judicial Committee of the Privy
Council, reversing the decision of the Court of the Arches, held

have in effect operated as charters of liberty to
Evangelicals and to Anglo-Catholics respectively as
touching matters of sacramental belief ; and that
both judgments were the work of a wholly Erastian
tribunal, which in the former of the two cases
reversed the decision previously given by the Church
courts. It can be pointed out, further, that the new
instrument of synodical discipline, recently devised
by the Bishops, however convenient in practice, is
easily capable of being misused. A Bishop who
commands the respect of his clergy will in practice
be able, in almost all cases, to secure a majority—
perhaps an overwhelming majority—in support of
his policy. It requires courage, as well as thought-out
conviction, to oppose the policy of the Bishop in
synod ; nor will it in all cases be easy in practice, it
is to be feared, for the clergy to exclude wholly from
their minds the consideration that the Bishops
control a great deal of diocesan patronage. A
synodical vote means a majority decision, which can
then be employed to put strong moral (though not
legal) pressure upon those clergy (few, perhaps, in

that it was not contrary or oppugnant to the declared doctrine
of the Church of England to affirm that regeneration does not
invariably take place in Baptism, being conditional on worthy
reception ; the same tribunal in the case of Sheppard *v.* Bennett
held that it was not contradictory or repugnant to anything in
the Articles or Formularies of the Church to affirm a ' real,
actual, objective ' Presence of Christ in the Sacrament of Holy
Communion under the forms of Bread and Wine.

number) who belong to the dissentient minority, and to brand them as ' rebels '. It is a method of procedure which may be as easily employed to coerce and stigmatize ' heretics ' as to discourage and isolate what are described as liturgical or extra-liturgical irregularities. Expression was given last year by Canon Streeter, in a letter to *The Times*,[1] to the fear that the Church of England, if converted into ' a nice, tidy, smooth-running, little Church ', might be found, in the end, to exclude impartially the free criticism of the New Testament, the admission of Nonconformists to communion, and Latin devotions. ' Unfortunately ' (he added, quoting the words of a friend of his and of mine who was killed in the war) ' half the really live people want one or more of these things. Let them alone, they counter-act one another's excesses ; suppress them equally all round, and you have killed your Church.'

But the Church is killed equally, for all spiritual purposes, if it is subjected permanently in spiritual matters to the control of the State. The Church of England, at the time of the Reformation, accepted (no doubt under considerable pressure) both the Royal Supremacy and also some measure of Parliamentary control. But it was not at that time contemplated that the Royal supremacy should be

[1] *The Times*, Sept. 21, 1928.

put into commission, or that the Parliament which controlled the Church should include either non-Anglican members or the representatives of constituencies other than those in which the religion of the Church of England was established. Under modern conditions, the control of the Church in directly spiritual matters by a virtually secularised State has become an impossibility. A leading member of the Reformed Church of Switzerland, Dr. Adolf Keller, in a letter published in *The Times* of November 19, 1928, quotes some striking words of the Lutheran lawyer, Dr. Simons, President of the Supreme Court of Justice in Germany, who in a recent utterance remarked :—

' I confess to being a heretic as regards the ruling doctrine that all law derives its authority from the State. God is the source of the law, and has put bounds to the law of the State. When will the Church at last, taken as an unit, really " come of age " ? The maturity of the Church has been delayed by the institution of the State Church.

' The Church should remember what Luther said to his Prince : " I can better protect your Grace than you can protect me." She should not consider her autonomy as a constitutional right given to her by the State, but as a right the privilege of which was hers from birth.'

The Church, in a word, cannot really be killed, because the Church—unlike the State—is in the last resort a Society not of this world. Whatever may have been the case in the past, a Church controlled by the State in respect of directly spiritual concerns in the modern world is impossible. Neither the English Free Churchman nor the foreign Protestant nor our own fellow-Anglicans abroad have the least use for the Erastian idea under modern conditions. It belongs to a past age. And the risks of freedom, therefore, have to be taken. It may be hoped that the lessons of the past, as well as of the present, will in practice prove to have been learnt, and that the Church, if she regains or successfully asserts her own spiritual freedom, will refrain from converting herself into a sect. The Church here in England will achieve this result in proportion as she learns to think of the two provinces of Canterbury and York in relation to world-wide Anglicanism, and of the Anglican Communion as a whole in relation, not primarily to the confessional standards of an insular past, but to the theology and life of the Church of Christ upon the ecumenical scale.

For the Anglican Church, if on the one hand she no longer commands the full spiritual allegiance of the whole people of England,[1] has on the other hand

[1] Apart from the large minority of convinced Nonconformists

long ceased (as I began this lecture by remarking) to be in any specific or narrow sense English.   There are Anglicans who can speak no word of English, just as there are Anglicans who are the subjects, not of the British Crown, but of the Japanese Empire, or of the United States of America, or of the Portuguese or of the Chinese Republic.   If my calculations (based on reference to *Crockford*) are not incorrect, there are in the world to-day some 240 dioceses of the Anglican Communion, apart altogether from the four home countries of England, Ireland, Scotland, and Wales. The Lambeth Conference, when it assembles in 1930, may render its customary decennial service by reminding Englishmen (who still seem to need the reminder) of the world-wide scope and extension of the great religious communion to which so many of them still claim to belong ; and it is even possible that the domestic perplexities of the two original provinces of Canterbury and York may then come to be seen in their proper proportions.

(including, of course, Roman Catholics), it is a regrettable fact that a considerable proportion of the people of England is at the present time religiously indifferent. The actual strength of the Church of England is not easy to estimate. It has certainly failed to keep pace with the growth of the population. The Bishop of Durham (*op. cit.*, pp. 42 *seq.*) points out that, according to the latest official returns, out of a total population of over thirty-six millions, only 3,686,422 persons above the age of eighteen registered themselves in 1927 as members of the National Church, and that of these only 2,528,391 were communicants. In the time of James I there were 2,250,000 communicants out of a total population of about four millions.

What, then, do we mean by the Anglican Church? We mean, presumably, the Christian Church in communion with Canterbury, which, in its post-Reformation form, was for some centuries little more than an insular sect, tied and bound by the chains of the State, but which in more modern days has grown gradually into a world-wide communion, unestablished (except in the two original provinces), and accustomed to freedom : a Church in process of shaking off limitations, and of learning (more and more, in proportion as the modern religious outlook becomes more and more international) to think both of itself, and also of its theology and spiritual life, in relation not to Englishmen merely, but to mankind, and to the theology and life of the Church of Christ as an ecumenical whole.

In my first lecture I used the term ' Christendom ' : I shall be expected, of course, to define it. A definition in precise and clear terms is not easy. A traditional definition would be the whole body of christened (i.e., baptized) people ; but it is a definition which by implication would exclude (for example) the Society of Friends : and the Friends, having regard to their obvious and manifest Christianity, and despite their rejection of sacraments, it would be paradoxical in some sort not to include. There are other marginal cases ; there are semi-

Christian, or (at least) unorthodox, sects, and there are individuals too who in some sort are Christian, though (for whatever reason) unbaptized. I have myself used elsewhere the phrase ' ragged edges ' ; and there *are*, I think, ragged edges. There is a fringe of marginal cases. I should not myself be prepared to define with rigidity the limits of Christendom in any terms of exclusiveness. I should at least desire to include within the scope of the term all such persons as would be prepared, if it came to a question of martyrdom, to suffer martyrdom, side by side, for Christ's sake. And the ' noble army of martyrs ' has no denominational limits.

Professor N. P. Williams, of Oxford, in a recent pamphlet remarks that the modern student (the Professor himself has in mind more particularly the modern student of ' Anglo-Catholic ' convictions) ' tends to conceive the Church as a living and growing organism, rather than as a mechanism or a legal corporation.'[1] The conception of the Church (the Professor points out) which results from this line of thought is in effect that which is summed up in the phrase of the Anglican Bidding Prayer, ' Christ's holy Catholic Church—that is, the whole congregation of Christian people dispersed throughout the

[1] N. P. Williams, *Anglo-Catholicism : an Individual Impression*, p. 23.

whole world.' It is possible, no doubt, to 'regard
certain areas of this ecumenical " congregation " as
normally, and others as abnormally or defectively,
organised ',[1] and for Anglican Christians it is at least
natural to think of Episcopacy—the historic form
of Church order which they themselves have inherited
—as constituting the 'normal' form of Church
organisation. It is not desirable to surrender it. It
is certainly more than a merely convenient form of
Church government. It is a vital link with the
Christian Church of past ages, a link which reaches
back far behind all the existing divisions of Christendom, and of which the origins (whatever the
obscurities in detail of the earliest forms of incipient
Church order in the period of the New Testament and
in the sub-apostolic age which succeeded it) are at
least continuous in principle with the idea of the
ordering and government of the Church by Apostles
and other ministers 'sent' from Christ in New
Testament times.

Apart, moreover, from all those questions of origin
with regard to which there is room for legitimate
divergence of view amongst scholars,[2] it is to-day

[1] Williams, op. cit., p. 24.

[2] The latest work dealing specifically with the origins of the
Christian ministry is Canon Streeter's recently published Hewett
Lectures for 1928 on *The Primitive Church*, a brilliantly written
study in which, however, the writer inevitably makes free use of
his stimulating powers of conjecture. Canon Streeter believes

coming to be more and more widely acknowledged that the episcopal system of ministry (with whatever mitigation may be found necessary of its ' prelatical ' character, and with due regard for the values enshrined in other traditions) holds out the manifest promise and hope of the future, as being in effect the one conceivable form of Church order which could be accepted in practice for any proposed scheme of reunion upon an ecumenical scale. And reunion, in any organic sense, does mean, in respect of the future, an agreed form of Church order. I do not myself think that the hope of Christian reunion is really in the long run promoted by the policy (which in some quarters finds advocates) of immediate inter-communion with the adherents of other Church systems, upon the basis of ignoring or waiving the question of ministry. Organic and corporate reunion implies clearly agreement as to who is, or is not, entitled or authorised in practice to minister and to celebrate the Eucharist on behalf of the Church : and the principle of explicit authorisation to act in the name of Christ on behalf of the Church appears to be more adequately expressed and more adequately safeguarded by episcopal ordination

that the forms of ministry in the earliest age of Church History were various, and that, among these, ' the Episcopalian, the Presbyterian, and the Independent can each discover the prototype of the system to which he himself adheres.'

in the historic succession of the ministry than by other and (in some cases) more loosely-conceived ministerial systems. In the long run, and from the point of view of any hoped-for reunion, an eventually universal episcopate would appear to be the one possible form of Church order.[1]

To say this is not to deny—and it ought not to be held to involve the denial—that the sacraments, ministered outside the episcopal system, may be, and are, efficacious, from a spiritual point of view, in the case of those who in good faith receive them. To expect non-Anglicans, or non-Episcopalians, to be false to their own spiritual past by denying the validity of their ecclesiastical life is preposterous. There is no doubt a highly technical sense in which, from the point of view of traditional theology, ordinations outside the episcopal system may be, and are sometimes, described as ' invalid '. It was a principle which before the Reformation was generally recognised, at least from very early times, that a Bishop is the proper minister of ordination :

[1] The *Proposed Scheme of Union* prepared by the Joint Committee of the Church of India, Burma and Ceylon, the South India United Church, and the South India Provincial Synod of the Wesleyan Methodist Church, contemplates ultimately an universally episcopal Church. The scheme as it stands presents difficulties from the point of view of strict Anglicanism, more particularly as regards the interim period. It is understood that it is to be carefully discussed by the Bishops at Lambeth ; and it would be obviously wrong to prejudge the results of their lordships' discussion.

and this principle, wherever episcopacy was discarded, was of course broken through. But 'invalid', in this technical sense, does not mean, and should not be taken to mean, 'spiritually inefficacious'. The term 'invalid', as popularly used and (like other technical terms) popularly misunderstood, is misleading ; it is apt to suggest what is plainly untrue, namely, that the sacraments of those who in good faith stand outside the episcopal system of order are in a spiritual sense null and void ; and we have no kind of right to say that. Negative dogmatisms are, in a case of this kind, inadmissible. There is owed by all Christians towards all portions of Christendom the indispensable obligation and duty of charity. It is the first and most necessary step towards future reunion that there should arise throughout Christendom a generation deliberately trained to observe this duty, and to abstain, therefore, from modes of thought and of speech which are out of line with the Apostolic ideal of ' truth-speaking in love '. The problems of reunion are not easy. They are not to be solved in a one-sided manner, or at the cost of creating new schisms. Mutual respect, mutual sympathy, patience, the synthetic mind, perhaps also a new form of controversy, of which the aim is not dialectical victory but the real inner understanding of differences—all these things are required. And it is necessary, moreover, to look not to the Protestant world only, but to the Catholic world also.

A friend of my own, who had for some time resided in Germany, remarked in connexion, not long ago, with the Lausanne Conference which discussed ' Faith and Order ', that if the English Church could with real unanimity stand boldly before the world for the ideal of a free, modern, genuinely liberal Catholicism, there would be all over Europe a widespread and eager response. To such a suggestion the reply must be, I think, ' Yes ; but with the qualification that the proposed free, modern, and liberal Catholicism must be shown to be, and must succeed actually in being, at the same time, and in a genuine and full sense, Evangelical.' It is not merely the case that there is an Evangelical moment in Christianity, to which Catholicism in its traditional forms has not always done justice. The Evangelical moment is in a real sense primary : it is the essential ' new thing ' of the Gospel. The Reformation, on its positive side (I am thinking now more particularly of the Continental Reformation), did stand—as I cannot but think—for a largely new, as well as a positive and liberating, apprehension of the astonishing miracle of the free grace of God in redemption, as against what was really the over-legalised and relatively unevangelical Christianity of the Latin Church of the period. There is something, I believe, to be learnt from the Lutheran tradition—perhaps even from the Calvinist tradition : and the Roman Church has not learnt it. It was the defect, too, of the English Tractarians that, in their reaction from Protestantism, they exclusively looked to the past. They became theological archaists, their conceptions both of the Church and of Christian theology were static, and for all practical purposes they were content virtually to ignore the whole Protestant witness. They were, at least in some cases, in danger, as the Roman Church is in danger, of being un-evangelical.

A free, modern, and genuinely evangelical, as well as genuinely liberal, Catholicism—that means think-ing in terms of the whole. It means the deliberate attempt to get away from whatever is partial, limited, narrow, accidental, or insular, a deliberate readiness to sit loose to whatever is in a merely denominational sense Anglican, in order to com-prehend whatsoever is in a legitimate and real sense Christian. A true Catholicism will be truly synthetic. It will embrace, with elastic charity, a rich profusion of elements, and it will do so not on a basis of legalism, but with real largeness and freedom of mind. The test by which it will seek to regulate itself will be the test of conformity, not so much to the letter, as to the general spirit, of its regulations and rules. It will seek to work towards a community of mind of which the basis shall be not coercion, but freedom of consent. It will employ the discipline, not of force, but of suasion. It will not seek to override or to drive out minorities, and it will recognise elements of religious practice derived from all quarters, upon the sole condition that whatsoever finds recognised or officially tolerated place in its synthesis must be capable of penetration by the authentic spirit of the Gospel.

Of the emergence of such a type of Catholicism the Anglican Church, in its modern development, holds out the best hope. Between the four main confessional types of Christianity—Latin, Orthodox, Lutheran, and Calvinistic (or Reformed)—Anglicanism occupies historically an intermediate position. It has points of connexion, affinities, contacts, with them all ; but it is at once its strength and its peculiarity that it has never, in the course of its post-Reformation development, been identified fully or completely with any one of the four. It is the clear vocation of the Anglican Church in the world of to-day, in relation to all the various inter-confessional movements and aspirations after unity with which Christendom is astir, to play the part of a mediator ; to hold out hands, and, as between different types of tradition, to build bridges of understanding : to attempt to learn from them all : to incorporate values derived from all quarters : and to enrich and deepen its own spiritual life by so doing.

Of the four types I have mentioned, the tradition of Latin Christianity must no doubt, in relation to the Church of England, on historical grounds be placed first. The Christianity of the West represents in a real sense, in the first instance, the ' hole of the pit ' whence we were ' digged ' ; and the tradition of Latin theology underlies much that is characteristic of Anglicanism, though in scholarly Anglicanism the influence of the Greek patristic tradition has been almost equally strong. Religiously speaking, the Latin tradition primarily means S. Augustine, the influence of whose writings and mind upon the whole subsequent mind and religious life of the Latin Church was profound. The Latin theology of more recent times is the heir, not of Augustine alone, but of the schoolmen. It has tended to legalism. It has believed in sharp, clear-cut distinctions—the distinction, for example, between religion as ' natural ' and religion as ' revealed ',[1] and the corresponding

[1] For a criticism of this see C. C. J. Webb, *Problems in the Relations between God and Man*, pp. 49 *seqq.*

H

distinction between the natural and the supernatural
' orders ', alike of truth and of being.   It has believed
also in supernaturally-authorised organs of infallibility—the Bible, the Church, and the Pope.   Latin
Christendom, from a devotional point of view, has
been enormously rich, manifold, and passionate ;
and we have, in my judgment, a great deal to learn
both from the lives of its saints and from its devotional
and spiritual traditions—in some cases also from its
devotional methods, in respect both of worship and
of prayer.   Apart, moreover, from the massive
structure of mediæval systematic theology (which
still merits study), there are contemporary intellectual
movements within the Latin Church of to-day—a
considerable output of scholarly theology, especially
in Germany, Belgium, and France ; and, in southern
Germany, a peculiarly interesting ' liturgical movement '.   We can, and should, learn from the Latin
tradition.   But we shall abjure, if we are wise, Roman
legalism, Roman infallibility, and the Roman tradition of exclusiveness ; and we shall abstain also, if
we are wise, from taking over the minor superstitions
of Rome, such (for example) as the cultus of relics,
or the more exaggerated and indefensible forms of
devotion to the Mother of our Lord and to other saints.

The Greek, or Orthodox, tradition presents an
interesting contrast.   It differs widely from that of

the West. It conceives both of the Church, and of the nature of Christianity, in a quite different way. Russian and Greek Christianity is, no doubt, conservatively ' orthodox ', not merely in name, but in fact ; but its orthodoxy is certainly of a different type from our own. It conceives of the Church, not as a legal corporation, but as Christ's mystical Body, the Communion of Saints—a living organism, a fellowship of life, pulsing with the great joy of the resurrection of Christ, which it interprets as a great act of cosmic significance, transforming and glorifying the whole of Creation. The Eastern Church believes primarily not so much in the infallibility of the Church's mind as in the indefectibility of the Church's life. There are, to its thinking, no official organs of infallibility—the authority even of an ecumenical Council depends in the last resort, according to Eastern theologians, upon the endorsement of its decisions by the Church as a whole. The Church is hierarchical but not hierocratic. The highest authority in the Church is the whole Church, not the Bishops as such. According to Eastern theologians, the whole body of the faithful participates in the whole life of the Church ; the priesthood of the ordained clergy is to be interpreted in a ministerial and representative sense. The liturgical worship of the Church is to orthodox worshippers a profound spiritual mystery, at once ' symbolically realistic ' and ' realistically symbolic ', expressive of the mystically real fellowship of God with men and of the faithful one with another and with the whole communion of saints, past, present and to come, in the one Body of the Christ. The Church is before all things a fellowship of faith and love ; and humility and love are the two Christian virtues on which the piety of the Eastern Church sets most store.[1]

Of the Lutheran tradition, apart from its sixteenth-century origins, the Anglican theologians of the past have for the most part (to their shame) known very little. Biblical criticism, of course, has during the last three quarters of a century penetrated widely into Anglican circles ; and it has come to us, largely though of course not exclusively, from nominally Lutheran sources. It remains true that the *systematic* theology of the Lutheran Church, in its more modern forms, if we make exception for Ritschlianism (a by no means fully representative movement), has been almost wholly ignored.

The Lutheran emphasis is upon the ' Word ' of the Gospel—that is to say, upon the comforting message of God's free grace and love towards sinners. As the presupposed background of this there is the

[1] For the substance of the above paragraph I have made use of F. Zankow, *Das orthodoxe Christentum des Ostens* (Berlin, 1928), and N. Arseniew, *Mysticism and the Eastern Church* (S.C.M., 1926).

Scriptural doctrine of God's eternal antagonism, or 'wrath', against sin. Justification and judgment, together with the Gospel 'Word' of salvation through Christ from the power of sin, death, and the devil—these are the poles of the Lutheran religion, as they are to a large extent also the poles of the religion of S. Paul. It is claimed by Lutheran theologians that the new, or, at least, the revived, emphasis upon the 'Word' of the Gospel, which goes back to Luther, and which plays such a dominating part in their tradition, has a significance not merely for soteriology but christology, and indeed for the understanding of Christian theology as a whole. To have listened, as a small group of Anglicans in the summer of 1928 had the privilege of listening,[1] to a modern Lutheran theologian expounding systematically the doctrine of Christian salvation and of atonement through Christ, was to be convinced that we have something to learn from the Lutherans.

There is, lastly, the Calvinist tradition, akin to Lutheranism, and yet wholly distinct. It is in certain respects far more intensely theocratic than Lutheranism ; and it underlies, of course, Presbyterianism. The original Calvinist doctrines of predestination and election, of total depravity, and of what the brothers

[1] At the Wartburg Conference, at Eisenach, Thuringia, Germany, August 11-17, 1928.

Wesley described as the ' horrible decrees ', are to-day widely discredited, and are, no doubt, *prima facie* quite horrible. I am far from suggesting that Calvinism, in the original form, should be revived. But the Calvinist tradition in theology nevertheless does stand for an immense and salutary emphasis upon the uncreated majesty of God, and perhaps also for the recognition (indispensable to religion, as I think) of the element of mystery in God—the God whose thoughts are not our thoughts, and whose ways are not our ways, the God upon whom His creatures depend, but who in no way depends upon them. The new, paradoxical, stimulating, perhaps epoch-making, movement in continental theology which is associated with the names of Karl Barth, Emil Brunner, and Friedrich Gogarten, and of which more will be heard in this country eventually, is in a very real sense a revival, in certain respects, of the Calvinist tradition.

Distinct theologically, the four traditions thus briefly characterised are distinct also devotionally. The Roman liturgy, grave, dramatic, dynamic, deeply impressive, with its sober objectivity, its unemotional character, its emphasis upon the idea of the ' thing done ' before God, and its severe impersonality, has been described by a modern liturgical scholar as ' dogma ' (or ' truth ') ' turned into prayer '.[1]

[1] R. Guardini, *Vom Geist der Liturgie*, pp. 9 *seq.* : ' *Gebetete*

The Eastern, or Orthodox, liturgy is by contrast a great mystery-drama of adoration and glorification. ' A cloud of mystery surrounds the whole service . . . the liturgical acts . . . are, so to speak, coloured transparencies of the Divine majesty and glory.'[1] The part played by the people is, relatively speaking, receptive and passive : they stand in awed contemplation, at once rejoicing and shuddering, carried away, rapt into heaven, as it were, by the spirit of the divine drama of worship, adoration and praise which, veiled from sight by the *iconostasis*, is yet enacted before them. ' The whole conception of the Eastern service is dominated by that saying of the Johannine Jesus : " Whosoever believeth on me, *hath* eternal life, and *is passed* from death unto life." '[2] The Eastern Church in this liturgy ' truly possesses the treasure of the Gospel, and it only waits for a great evangelical awakening to reveal this treasure in all its splendour '.[3]

Diverse at once from the Eastern and from the Latin types of worship is the Lutheran type. It is directed and orientated not so much towards God, as towards man. It expresses the divine approach

towards man through the mediation of Christ, and
by means of the proclamation of the divine message
or ' Word ' of the Gospel. The ' Word of God '—
that is the central idea. Whether by means of the
sermon, or by means of the reading of Scripture, or
again by means of the Sacrament (which to Lutheran
minds is a kind of *verbum visibile*, a symbolical
confirmation or ' seal ' of the Gospel), the same
message is set forth—the glad tidings of God's free
love towards sinners. Prayer enters into the service,
but it is a prayer evoked by the ' Word ', the response
of man's heart to the Gospel assurance of blessed-
ness.

In strong contrast, once more, is the Calvinistic
conception of worship. Austere, puritan, stripped
bare of all symbolism, and dominated (according to
its original idea) by the dogma of predestination,
the Calvinist service exalts simply the glory of God.
I transcribe part of Heiler's account : ' To proclaim
God's glory, to praise and magnify it, to bow before
the awful majesty of God, and to make petition to
the King of Eternal Glory—that is the end and aim
which the Calvinistic service sets before it. *Soli Deo
gloria !*—the individual man, with his sin and misery
and his longing for salvation, becomes as nothing in
the splendour of God's majesty. He throws himself
down before Him in the deepest reverence, yea even

if God inflicts damnation upon him, for even in the lamentations of the damned God's glory is made manifest. Luther proclaims without ceasing, " To thee, to thee has God offered salvation " ; Calvin knows nothing of the individual, but only the great company of the Elect and Predestined, the holy People of God who are called to reign with God. Therefore the purpose of the service is not to bring the consolations of grace to the sin-laden soul ; it is a solemn act of homage on the part of the whole congregation. The whole community of believers comes before God to worship Him in His absolute Greatness and Glory. The place of meeting becomes a sanctuary or temple, in which God's Glory dwells, in which the congregation in deepest humility prays to its present Lord.'[1]

Now, the Anglican Church stands between all these traditions.[2] It is flexible. It has points of connexion

---

[1] Heiler, *op. cit.*, pp. 95 *seqq.*

[2] The Anglican liturgy of 1662, though of course it is capable of being understood in the ' receptionist ' sense characteristic of Calvinism, is from another point of view ultra-Latin. The form of the Consecration Prayer, with its abrupt ending, especially if read in the light of the form provided for a supplementary consecration, is apt to lend colour to the almost magical idea that the consecration of the elements for their sacred purpose is effected by means of the recital over them of the words, ' This is My Body ', ' This is My Blood ', as a kind of charm. The Scottish, American and South African liturgies are all superior, from this point of view, to the English. The form provided as an alternative in the Book of 1928, which proceeds, after an address of praise to the Father, to an *anamnesis* or commemoration of the work of the Son, and then to the prayer that God with His Holy and life-

with all of them. In the seventeenth century it narrowly escaped being a sect ; but it has to-day shaken itself free. It can play the part of a ' bridge-Church '. It possesses no doubt a central ' mind ' of its own, but that is not the whole truth about it. It has a fringe—or, indeed, a variety of fringes—of enthusiasts. It can, and does, make experiments—theologically, as well as liturgically. It is not strictly restrained within bounds.

It is precisely this characteristic which makes Anglicanism, from the point of view of all those who desire neatness, precision, discipline, unanimity, strict order—the ideal (in however mitigated a form) of the Roman Church, with its dragooned, disciplined, regimented, orderly Church life—so exceedingly elusive and baffling. That the central mind of the Anglican Church stands, as a whole, firmly and solidly for the central truths of the Gospel and for the main faith of Christendom generally—that is to say, for the Gospel of God's grace and love in Christ Jesus ; for the Trinity, the Incarnation, and the Atonement ; and (despite all minor divergences of doctrine and of detailed interpretation of these things)

giving Spirit may bless and sanctify the Eucharistic gifts that they may be unto us the Body and Blood of His Son our Saviour Jesus Christ, is conceived upon Eastern lines, and is from the point of view of theology and right reason an enormous improvement. A distinguished Lutheran has described it as ' the finest liturgy at present available for use in any part of Christendom.'

for the Church and the Sacraments—of this there can be no real question. But it is to-day more and more coming to be the case that the Anglican Church stands for these things on a basis of freedom. And that does mean anomalies. It means raggedness of edges, a great flexibility, a good deal of variety in worship and teaching, an occasional heretic. There are individual teachers within Anglicanism—men who, in some cases, occupy important positions—who, to judge by their utterances, depart in certain respects somewhat widely from the official mind of the Church. The Church deliberately tolerates them : but they are not to be regarded as being more representative of the general mind of the Church than they actually are. The proper reply to the cold *douche* of negation is not heresy-hunting, but constructive and positive teaching, based on reasoned conviction and scholarship. The witness borne by the central and positive mind of the Church is impressive in precise proportion as it is seen to represent not merely the voice of tradition, but the free consensus of living minds, nurtured, indeed, in faith, but engaged in thinking out freely the truths implied in their faith, and in the Christian faith generally.

The real curse of the Church at the present time— more especially in the two provinces of Canterbury and York—is the spirit of party, which (as the result primarily of the controversies raised with regard to the Prayer Book) has been temporarily stirred up afresh. There are Anglo-Catholics, and there are also Evangelicals, who are wholly reactionary, who appear to have learnt and forgotten little or nothing, and whose minds continue to move in past grooves. There is a wing of the Evangelicals which is narrow and bibliolatrous, polemical, stubbornly intolerant and bitter : and there is a wing of the Anglo-Catholics which is impossibly Roman—not indeed in the sense of acknowledging the Papacy, but in the sense of being Roman in principle, and in general temper of mind. The future does not belong to such people. It belongs in each case to the more liberal wing, which has made its count with the modern world and with modern methods of thought, and which knows how to distinguish the wood from the trees. Among those also who call themselves ' Modernists ' there are, it is to be feared, some few who are regrettably intolerant, narrow, obsolete in mind, representing not genuinely the living thought of to-day, but the high-and-dry liberalism of yesterday. The future, once more, does not belong to such people. The old party divisions, in a real atmosphere of freedom, might well be allowed to disappear altogether within a measurable distance of time, though there

will of course be room still for variety of outlook,
and for varying divergence of emphasis. The younger
educated clergy of all schools, in so far as they have
been theologically trained in a modern atmosphere
of thought, begin to-day to understand one another,
and to discover the possibilities, not merely of mutual
toleration, but of synthesis.

It is not to be denied that the Church in England
to-day suffers from manifest evils. There are those
who complain of a growing rift between clergy and
laity, and of a false clericalism on the part of many of
the former, sometimes manifesting itself in the form
of a doctrinaire and intolerant dogmatism, sometimes in the form of abrupt changes of ceremonial of
a kind which (it may be) are neither desired nor
understood by the people. The more ' extreme '
Anglo-Catholics, whose zeal, in particular districts
and circumstances, has in some cases outrun discretion, may be easily represented as an ' aggressive
and insolent faction ' ; though it is only fair to
remember that at least equal harm can be done by
the action of party ' trusts ' of a different kind, which
in some cases have purchased for money the right to
present clergy to livings with the express purpose of
bringing about changes no less abrupt, and no less
disliked by the people, in a different direction.

The evils complained of are real ; but they are

not confined to one 'school of thought'. The variations which at present exist between parish and parish are often wide, and in 'single-church areas' may be of such a kind as to afford grounds for a legitimate grievance on the part of the convinced adherents of 'schools of thought' for whose needs the clergy are failing to cater. The difficulty in urban areas, in which variety of parishes exists, is less seriously felt. The remedy is in any case not to be sought (or, at least, it is not to be found) in the idea of strictly enforceable limits of a clearly-defined, hard and fast kind, within which alone variations of use would be sanctioned. The revised Prayer Book of 1928 suggests, no doubt, and was meant to suggest, an approved limit of variation, within which, for the sake of order and peace, it may be hoped that existing practice, so far as is reasonably feasible, will for the present be brought. But it is obvious that, in particular cases, the traditions and spiritual life of a parish may be (and are sometimes) destroyed, and the laity alienated, as the result of the abrupt introduction, in either of two possible directions, of changes in methods of worship which would fall well within the limits proposed. On the other hand, some at least of those clergy who have been accustomed in practice to go beyond the proposed limits have the active support of their laity ; and apart from this, it is important to recognise that in some cases (though not in all) they are by no means narrow obscurantists; that among their number must be included a certain proportion of not wholly unrepresentative Anglicans, who are capable of being in mind and theology quite modern, and in pastoral relationships tactful, fair-minded, and reasonable men.

The real harm, it may be suggested, is brought about not so much by the mere fact of the existence of variations (even wide variations) of churchman-ship, as by clerical autocracy; in part, no doubt, also as the result of the unsatisfactory working of the Anglican system (or lack of system) as regards patronage;[1] and in part, perhaps, in some cases by the existence of an attitude of needless suspicion in the minds of some members of the laity. To the end of time some human beings, and among them some clergy, will be lacking in wisdom. Sympathetic administration and pastoral guidance, wisely and tactfully given on the part of the Bishops, can do something to help. The troubles which afflict the Church, in so far as they are curable, can be otherwise

[1] A 'Benefices (Patronage) Measure', at present under con-sideration by the Church Assembly, has encountered much adverse criticism, and its ultimate fate is uncertain. It is to be hoped that effect will in any case be eventually given to the main principle of the Measure—that the laity of the parish concerned should be in some way consulted before an appointment is finally made.

cured, I would suggest, in two ways—by the inculcation of a spirit of pastoral charity and tact in the clergy themselves, and (most important of all) by the making of provision, upon a really effective scale, for their more adequate education.

The problem of the supply, education, and training of the future clergy of the Church is beyond question the most serious and the most immediately urgent of all the problems by which the Church of England is at present confronted. The average age of the English clergy is now said to be no less than 57 years : there are about four thousand fewer clergy at work in the parishes than was the case before the war ; and the numbers ordained year by year are, despite recent efforts, insufficient still to balance even numerically the annual losses by death or retirement. The facts are well known, and have been frequently stated. There are still few signs of any attempt, on the part of the Church as a whole, to handle the problem in any effective or adequate way. There appears, year by year, in the Budget of the Church Assembly the item ' Training for the Ministry : New Candidates—£20,000 ' ; but it stands low down in the list of items, and in practice it represents only a token vote—an aspiration which is not fulfilled. There is an annual deficiency on the Budget, and the item in question is never reached. The amount actually contributed by central Church funds for the training of candidates for the ministry is at present nothing at all.

On the other hand, by the individual Boards of Finance in the dioceses a certain amount is contributed locally : the sums so spent in the year 1928 are said to have reached a total of £24,600. Of the theological colleges the majority are in a position to assist some of their candidates by the offer of small bursaries ; and there exist also funds, of varying and undisclosed amount, which are raised and administered under the auspices of particular ecclesiastical organisations of a more or less ' party ' kind. There is, besides these, the Sponsors Scheme, for which the Church is indebted to the initiative of Earl Grey, and for which appeals are periodically made in the Press. Under this scheme about £60,000 has been contributed or promised within the course of the last two years.[1] It is none the less true that the needs of the Church in this matter are not being effectively met upon anything approaching an adequate scale. There is no dearth of candidates, potential and actual. But there is a real dearth of funds even appreciably adequate to endow them and to provide for their training ; and moreover, if the

[1] Earl Grey's speech in the Church Assembly, June 19, 1929 (see Church Assembly *Report of Proceedings*, Vol. X, No. 2, p. 274).

I

requisite funds were available, and if the desired rapid increase in the number of candidates under training took place, it would quickly become manifest that there is a real dearth also of suitable teachers and students of theology for the adequate staffing of the university faculties and theological colleges which would then be required.

The existing theological colleges, and even the faculties of theology at the Universities, are at the present time not too well staffed. At the leading Universities there is, of course, a supply of teachers of first-rate calibre, though their numbers are small, and they are apt to have too much to do. The theological colleges are, for the most part, on too small a scale ; they provide, very often, an opportunity for devotional training, but they are intellectually weak. The principals of these colleges are, in the majority of cases, struggling heroically, under almost impossible conditions, to impart a real education, and in many instances also to prevent that education from being unduly partisan. The results are not satisfactory. Every Examining Chaplain knows that the Church of England at the present time ordains annually to its ministry a certain proportion of candidates who are ill-educated, badly-equipped, and deficient in knowledge and in experience of the world. It is hard to reject candidates, when the needs are so great. A Church, nevertheless, which persists in ordaining candidates of the type indicated has no moral right to complain at a subsequent stage because its clergy are not always wise.

It has been pointed out by the Bishop of Durham[1] that an increasing proportion of the clergy is being drawn, and will in the future be drawn, from those ranks of society which have not hitherto been accustomed to send their sons to the universities and public schools, and which are in fact quite unable to do so. ' Humbly-born ' candidates of the ' artisan class ' are in a large number of cases most admirable material, and are capable in many instances of profiting by the very finest education which the Church has it within its power to bestow. Their *initial* social and educational background is of necessity limited. They need not less, but much more, spent on their education and training than do candidates of what used to be the more conventional type. The Bishop of Manchester, speaking in the Church Assembly in June, 1929, estimated the average cost to the Church of a candidate subsidised under the Sponsors Scheme at £250. It is evident that in the case of not a few of the more ' humbly-born ' candidates the figure proposed should be very

[1] In a speech made in the Church Assembly, June 19, 1929.

much higher. A really first-rate education costs
from £1000 to £1250. What would be thought of
a medical man upon whose training and education
no more than £250 had been spent ?

The problems of the supply and of the education
of candidates in sufficient numbers eventually to
make good the deficiency in the depleted ranks of the
ministry are not insoluble ; but they are not at
present being solved. There is need of a much larger
effort, conceived upon really statesmanlike lines. It
is a problem not simply of numbers, but of quality,
character and costliness of education and training.
Attention needs, in particular, to be directed not
merely to the supply of candidates, but to the supply
also of adequately trained theologians and teachers.
The conditions of parish life at the present time are
not favourable to the increase of learning, and the
few positions of relative leisure in the Church are
not always well used. Promising scholars should be
sought out and given real leisure and endowment for
scholarship, on the strict condition that they should
really engage in it. Teachers need to be subsidised
and recruited, as well as students ; and a higher
standard of general learning and scholarly competence on the part of those who are to be entrusted
with the training of candidates might well be secured.
There is need of a really imaginative appeal, boldly

framed, launched by the highest authorities of the
Church, backed by the whole of their influence,
pressed home with the utmost urgency upon the
conscience of the Church as a whole, and combined
with the promise that the money shall be administered in a large-minded and statesmanlike way, for
the raising of a large capital sum for the two-fold
purpose of the endowment of learning and the
training of candidates for the ministry. Only so can
the reproach which at present rests upon the Church
of England of being the one Christian community
which fails to provide full financial assistance for all
suitable candidates for its ministry be effectively
rolled away.

The future of the Anglican Church, despite all her
defects, sins, and follies, is potentially glorious, and
her vocation superb. In common with other portions
of Christendom, she draws her strength from divine
sources ; and the possibilities of renewed and revived
spiritual life are incalculable. None of her sons and
daughters has the least cause either to be ashamed
or to despair of her heritage. On the contrary, I
would, for my own part, endorse and adopt as my
own some words recently written, and with Canon
Raven, of Liverpool, I would say that the Church of
England, with all its defects, ' has stood always for
a reasonable faith, for the right to revise and
reinterpret, for the importance of sound learning.

It has cast off allegiance to infallibilities, has held out hands of welcome . . . to the scientist and the social reformer, and has been on the whole the champion of liberty and education. In the last twenty years it has developed enormously ; liberal views are characteristic of all the vital elements in its various parties ; it is becoming conscious of a new unity and solidarity, and a new type of Anglican at once evangelical, modernist, and catholic is emerging. It has done more than any other denomination to promote the passage from the old order to the new, has been singularly generous to the impatient among its own members in permitting experiments in doctrinal restatement and liturgical reform, has received a mass of more or less friendly criticism in penitence and hope, acknowledging freely the measure of its failure, and striving, in spite of its connexion with the State and the obscurantism of its extremists, to set its house in order.'[1]

I believe that the Anglican Church does hold out its hands to the future ; though in the end (but that is perhaps in the still distant future, hid from the eyes of to-day, and as may be determined by the eventual counsels of God) it will have to cease to be Anglican, and to become simply Christian— merged in the wider unity of the larger Christendom that shall one day be.

[1] C. E. Raven, *A Wanderer's Way*, p. 168.

APPENDICES

APPENDIX I

THE Archbishops and Bishops at the July sessions of the respective Convocations of the Provinces of Canterbury and York, 1929, submitted the following statement for the consideration of the Lower Houses, at the same time intimating that it would be proposed in the Upper Houses for adoption as a formal Resolution :—

' The worship of God is in every generation a primary concern of the Church. For many years the Church of England has been engaged in an endeavour to amend the existing laws of public worship so as to make fuller provision for the spiritual needs of the Church and to bring order into the variety of usage which has become prevalent. This endeavour has for the present failed. It is impossible and undesirable to bring back the conduct of public worship strictly within the limits of the Prayer Book of 1662. Accordingly the Bishops, having failed to secure the statutory sanction which was desired and sought, are compelled in the present difficult situation to fulfil by administrative action their responsibility for the regulation of public worship.

' On September 29, 1928, the Bishops announced that they intended to consult the clergy and laity of their dioceses. These consultations have now been held in almost every diocese, and in view of the information gained and desires expressed, the Bishops hereby resolve that in the exercise of their administrative discretion they will in their respective dioceses consider the circumstances and needs of parishes severally, and give counsel and directions. In these directions the Bishops will conform to the principles which they have already laid down, namely—

' (1) That during the present emergency and until further order be taken the Bishops, having in view the fact that the Convocations of Canterbury and York gave their assent to the proposals for deviations from and additions to the Book of 1662, as set forth in the Book of 1928, being laid before the National Assembly of the Church of England for Final Approval and that the Assembly voted Final Approval to these proposals, cannot regard as inconsistent with loyalty to the principles of the Church of England the use of such additions or deviations as fall within the limits of these proposals. For the same reason, they must regard as inconsistent with

loyalty to the principles of the Church of England
the use of any other deviations from or additions to
the Forms and Orders contained in the Book of
1662.

' (2) That accordingly the Bishops, in the exercise
of their legal or administrative discretion, will be
guided by the proposals set forth in the Book of 1928,
and will endeavour to secure that practices which
are consistent neither with the Book of 1662 nor
with the Book of 1928 shall cease.

' Further—

' (3) That the Bishops, in the exercise of their
authority, will only sanction the ordinary use of any
of the Forms and Orders contained in the Book
of 1928 if they are satisfied that such use would
have the goodwill of the people as represented in the
Parochial Church Council and that in the case of the
Occasional Offices the consent of the parties concerned will always be obtained.'

The above resolution was formally moved in the
Upper House of Convocation of York and was
carried *nemine contradicente*. In the Upper House
of Convocation of Canterbury it was carried by a
large majority, but with one very important amendment, viz. : the substitution for the words ' the
Church of England ' in the last sentence of the
paragraph numbered (1) of the words, ' Church

Order ', so that the sentence, in its amended form, ran ' For the same reason, they must regard as inconsistent with loyalty to the principles of *Church Order* the use of any other deviations from or additions to the Forms and Orders contained in the Book of 1662.'

The resolution, considered as a whole, is an admirable statement of a line of policy which, in the peculiar circumstances of the present time, must be regarded as wholly inevitable ; but the sentence which in the Canterbury form of the resolution was amended is, in its unamended original form, quite indefensible. There are a large number of possible ' deviations from or additions to the Forms and Orders contained in the Book of 1662 ' which do not fall within the limits of the proposals contained in the Book of 1928, and which nevertheless have been, and are, used in particular cathedrals or parish churches within the two provinces. Among such variations, there are some which are significant of presumptive variations in doctrine, while others are not. In neither case is it justifiable to affirm without qualification that those who make use of them must of necessity be regarded as being disloyal to ' the principles of the Church of England '; though, in view of the Bishops' statement of policy, they may, if and in so far as they refuse to comply with the new episcopal directions, be described not unfairly as being disloyal to ' the principles of Church Order '.

It is probable that what the Bishops had more particularly in mind was the ' extra-liturgical ' cultus of Christ in the Sacrament. The official and corporate mind of the Church of England, as for the time being expressed in the revised Prayer Book, disallows and would prohibit this practice ; and it is, indeed, obvious that it could not at the present time be given official or recognised sanction in either of the two English provinces with the general approval either of theologians or of the communicant laity. Regard for Church Order suggests, therefore, that it should not, in these circumstances, be introduced ; and that, in parishes where it already exists, it should, in the interests of order and peace, so far as possible by consent be abandoned.

But the matter is wholly a question of order. It is not a question of loyalty or of disloyalty to ' the principles of the Church of England ' ; for the Church of England is not, as a matter of fact, on the points at issue unanimous. There are dioceses and provinces of the Anglican Communion in which the type of devotion in question is, if not officially encouraged, at least tolerated, and in some cases sanctioned. It has been defended by Anglican

theologians of repute, and it has been explicitly
recognised by so high an authority as that of the
Bishop of Gloucester that those who seek to promote
it are in the majority of cases men to whose outlook
the terms ' idolatry ' and ' superstition ' are ' not
applicable '.[1]

The matter is still in a real sense under discussion
in the Church.   The cultus in question is widely
distrusted.   It is regarded in many quarters as being
' undesirable ' or ' dangerous ', and it has been
criticised on theological grounds.   But it finds also
defenders.   It is certainly a form of devotion to
Christ.   And it does not, in itself, appear of necessity
to involve any doctrine beyond (at the most) an
assertion of the ' real, actual, objective ' presence of
Christ in the sacrament—a form of belief which in
the Church of England is held very widely, and the
compatibility of which with ' the principles of the
Church of England ' has been explicitly upheld in
the Courts.

[1] *Reservation : Report of a Conference held at Farnham Castle
on October* 24–27, 1925, p. 135.

S. THOMAS AQUINAS, apart from the elaborate
discussion in which in the *Summa Theologica* he
worked it out in terms of the theory (to modern
thinking philosophically obsolete) of Transubstantiation, has given superb and classical expression to
the central faith of Christendom with regard to the
Eucharist in the great hymn *Lauda, Sion, Salvatorem*.
The stanza which affirms the ' Real Presence ' may
be quoted. It runs as follows :—

> ' Sub diversis speciebus,
> Signis tantum, et non rebus,
> Latent res eximiae ;
> Caro cibus, sanguis potus,
> Manet tamen Christus totus
> Sub utraque specie.'

The words mean that the two ' species ' or ' kinds '
in the Sacrament, the Bread and the Wine, are
' signs ' merely, which are to be distinguished from
the spiritual ' realities ' which they at once represent
and convey : the ' realities ' are the Body and Blood

of Christ : and yet Christ is not divided, but remains whole and entire beneath either ' species ' or ' kind '.

The distinction between ' sign ' and ' reality ' (*signum* and *res*) was traditional. Later mediæval theology distinguished, further, the *virtus* (i.e. the ' virtue ', or efficacy) of the sacrament. The Catechism in the English Prayer Book preserves the same threefold distinction between the ' outward part ', the ' inward part, or thing signified ', and the ' benefits ' of the sacrament. Further, the various post-Reformation divergences of doctrine become intelligible when they are seen in relation to these mediæval distinctions ; the purely symbolist view, commonly associated with the teaching of Zwingli, affirms that the sacrament is merely a *signum* ; the ' virtualist ' or ' receptionist ' view asserts that it is not merely a *signum* but an *efficax signum*, a means of divine grace which in effect conveys to those who rightly receive it the *virtus* or efficacy of Christ's Body and Blood ; while those who affirm doctrines of the ' Real Presence ' go further, and acknowledge the actuality and objectivity in the sacrament of the *res sacramenti*, or ' thing signified '.

The doctrine of the Real Presence is, nevertheless, full of difficulty. It can be affirmed only in paradoxes. Christ, say the theologians, is not in the sacrament ' as in a place '. To quote Cardinal

Newman, ' our Lord . . . neither descends from
heaven upon our altars, nor moves when carried in
procession. The visible species change their position,
but He does not move. He is in the Holy Eucharist
after the manner of a spirit. We do not know how.'
It is not surprising that the late Father Tyrrell, in
a well-known passage in *Through Scylla and Charybdis*
should speak of ' all the joy and reality ' as having
been ' taken out of a life that fed on devotion to
the Sacramental Presence ' as the result of a ' flash
of theological illumination ' with regard to the real
meaning of the orthodox doctrine on the subject.[1]
The question arises whether it may not be possible
to reach an improved form of doctrine.

' The danger of the word " Presence " ' (so the
present Bishop of Manchester is reported as having
remarked in the course of the discussion at Farnham
in 1925 on Reservation) ' is its connotation of absence
at other times '.[2] Those, of course, who affirm their
belief in the Real Presence would simply deny that
their doctrine involves this connotation. They would
discriminate different senses and meanings of the
term ' presence '. They would affirm, with the
Evangelicals and with the whole of the Christian
tradition, that Christians are at all times and in all

[1] G. Tyrrell, *op. cit.*, p. 100.
[2] *Reservation : Report of a Conference held at Farnham Castle
on October* 24–27, 1925, p. 43.

K

places in the presence of Christ, that they are never spiritually estranged from Him save by wilful and deliberate disloyalty and indulgence in sin, that at all times and in all places it is possible to hold fellowship with Christ through the Spirit, that the whole Christian life is a life which is lived spiritually ' in Christ '. They would nevertheless desire to affirm that there is in a real sense a special presence of Christ which is objectively mediated through the sacramental elements of Bread and Wine, which in virtue of their consecration are no longer *mere* Bread and *mere* Wine, but have become for faith's discernment in a real though mysterious sense Christ's Body and Christ's Blood. They would affirm that what faith discerns in the Eucharist is not something which is imaginary, but something that is real ; and they would claim that in the consecrated Host and in the contents of the chalice Christ is present in the eternal reality of His glorified manhood, appropriable through communion as the spiritual sustenance of Christian souls, rightly adored (even apart from communion) as the Lamb slain for us men from the foundation of the world.

There are, nevertheless, difficulties connected with the doctrine. I need not go into them. But it is clear that what is really at stake in the controversy is the affirmation of the actuality and objectivity in

the sacrament of the *res sacramenti*—Christ's Body
and Blood. As early as the time of the Fourth
Gospel the difficulty seems to have been felt that the
Christian language about ' eating the flesh ' and
' drinking the blood ' of Christ appeared cannibalistic
and crude,[1] and there are forms of the 'Real Presence'
doctrine in which a refined form of cannibalism
appears still to be latent. The explanation which in
the Fourth Gospel (after the harsh-sounding doctrine
has first been re-affirmed in its full paradox to the
crowd of Jews in the synagogue)[2] is eventually given
to the disciples would appear to suggest that it is
really the ' spirit ' and ' life ' of the risen and
ascended Christ (the ' Son of Man ' who has been
seen ' ascending where he was before ') which must
be held to constitute the true *res sacramenti*, the
inner reality which the Eucharist mediates.[3]

The present Master of Corpus Christi College,
Cambridge, (Mr. W. Spens), has suggested of late a
revised form of the ' Real Presence ' doctrine which
deserves, I think, to be carefully studied.[4]   It
appears to avoid many difficulties ; and provided
that in the end it is found to be satisfying to those
who, for want of a better word, must be called
Anglo-Catholics, it may well have the effect, in the

[1] John vi, 52.
[2] John vi, 53–59.   [3] John vi, 60–63.
[4] *Essays Catholic and Critical*, pp. 439 *seqq*.

end, of providing the basis of a possible Eucharistic irenicon between ' Catholics ' and ' Evangelicals ' in the Church.

Mr. Spens, at an earlier stage in his essay than that which discusses directly the Real Presence, raises the question why it was that theology could not in the case of the Eucharist remain content (as in the case of the sacrament of Baptism) with the recognition, side by side with the ' sign ' or ' sacrament ' itself, of the *virtus sacramenti* or ' benefits ', but must needs insist also upon the further discrimination of the *res sacramenti* as a third element involved.[1] The answer he finds (rightly, no doubt) in the words which at the Last Supper our Lord is said to have used—the words ' This is My Body ' and ' This is My Blood '. There is no parallel to these words in the case of the sacrament of Baptism ; and there is accordingly no insistence in the Christian tradition upon the idea of a ' consecration ' of the water—though, no doubt, in the majority of Christian Baptismal rites, including the forms prescribed in the Prayer Books of 1662 and 1928, there is some kind of a ' blessing ' or ' sanctification ' of the water—comparable in any way with the strong emphasis which has certainly been laid upon the idea of a ' consecration ' of the elements of Bread and

[1] Spens, *op. cit.*, p. 430.

Wine in the Holy Communion. There is in Baptism what may be described as an ' effectual symbolism of action '. In the Eucharist there is an effectual symbolism of action *which involves also what is described in Mr. Spens' terminology as an ' effectual symbolism of objects '*.

By an ' effectual ' symbol (as distinguished from a symbol which is purely didactic or dramatic) is meant a symbol which does not merely convey a message, but effects a result. A case in point would be token coinage, or paper money. A florin, once issued as such by the Mint, possesses a purchasing value in excess of its intrinsic value as bullion, and the value thus given to it is a ' real ' value, guaranteed by the State, and capable of effecting results : so that a florin is actual legal tender for two shillings, and a collection of ten such coins can be exchanged for a sovereign in actual gold. Similarly, a pound note, considered simply as paper, is virtually value- less ; but a pound note, considered from the point of view of the value given to it by a determination of the will of the State, is an ' effectual symbol ' of a pound sterling—it has the same purchasing power, it is legal tender for that amount, and we rightly and intelligibly speak of it, in the ordinary course of conversation, not as ' a piece of elaborately printed paper ', but as ' a pound '. ' The essence of such symbolism ', writes Mr. Spens, ' is the association of certain results or opportunities with certain visible signs by a will which is competent to bring about those results or give those opportunities ' ; and it is clearly within the competence of the will of the State to invest tokens, intrinsically valueless, with a specified purchasing power which will be valid at least within the ambit of the territorial dominions of the State in question.

Now, in the case of the Eucharist, the authority which (from the point of view of Christian belief) invests the elements of Bread and Wine with a significance, character and potency which did not belong to them before is not a will which (like that of a human society or state) is sovereign in a merely relative sense : it is a will which is in an *absolute* sense sovereign, the same will by which, in the first instance, the ' natural ' properties of the Bread and Wine were determined, viz. : the will of God, which is in an absolute sense ' competent ' to ' bring about the results and to give the opportunities ' which in the sacrament of Holy Communion are in view.

' In the case of the Eucharist,' writes Mr. Spens, ' the bread and the wine are given by Christ's ordinance[1] new properties, which, while they do not

[1] If the view were held, upon critical grounds, that our Lord at the Last Supper was not consciously instituting a rite for

annihilate the natural properties of giving sustenance and refreshment, yet so supersede these that we can rightly speak of the objects themselves as being changed and transfigured.'[1] The Bread and the Wine, in other words, from the moment of their consecration as media of the appointed sacrament, have become, for Christian faith, instinct, by a determination of the sovereign will of Almighty God, with a wholly new meaning and potency, a new character, a new set (as it were) of capacities and properties. They have become from henceforward the effectual symbols of Christ's Body and Blood, capable (as bread and wine, unconsecrated, are *not* capable) of mediating all that is meant and involved in eucharistic communion with Christ. In Mr. Spens' phrase, they have acquired ' a new property, namely, that their devout reception secures and normally conditions participation in the blessings of Christ's sacrifice, and therefore in His life '.[2] In *this* sense they have become, *without any connotation of materialism and also without any implication of cannibalism*, Christ's Body and Christ's Blood.

The elements, upon this view, have become (in

future observance, it would be necessary to re-write this sentence, and to substitute for ' Christ's ordinance ' the words ' the will of the Spirit, operating through the Church, i.e., ultimately by the sovereign will of God ', etc.

[1] Spens, *op. cit.*, p. 429.   [2] Spens, *op. cit.*, p. 441.

the sense indicated) Christ's Body and Blood
' *simply in and through their becoming effectual symbols.*'
An effectual symbol is rightly described (as we saw
in the case of the pound note) not in terms of its
original and natural properties, but in terms rather
of its new and acquired significance and efficacy, i.e.,
in terms of the reality which it effectually symbolises.
If this holds good even in the case of a piece of paper,
which by a determination of the will of the State
has the significance and efficacy of a pound sterling,
a fortiori it holds good in the case of the eucharistic
gifts, which by a determination of the will of
Almighty God have the significance and efficacy of
the Body and Blood of Christ. For the new spiritual
significance and efficacy of the elements in their
sacramental capacity is no less real than their
original character and significance as merely natural
objects ; it has the same ultimate basis (viz. : a
determination of the Divine Will) ; and it is obviously, from the point of view of religion, of much
greater importance. ' Such considerations,' remarks
Mr. Spens, ' justify the tendency to speak of the
consecrated elements as Host and Chalice, or as the
Blessed Sacrament, or, using our Lord's words, to
describe them as His body and blood, not as asserting
any material or quasi-material identity with His
natural or glorified body and blood, but as asserting

that they render Him appropriable as our sacrifice.'[1]
The natural properties of the bread and wine, considered simply *as* bread and wine, remain wholly
unchanged ; but they are from henceforward, from
the point of view of religion, irrelevant. What is
significant about the elements *now* is that they have
become the potential media of communion, that they
are (in the sense indicated, though not, of course, in
any other sense) the Body and Blood of Christ.

As such, moreover, they are adapted also to afford
what Christian devotion—at least in the case of those
to whom worship of an ' objective ' type is congenial
—appears to demand, namely, not a localised
presence, in time and in space, of the Lord who is
in no localised sense either in space or in time, but
what may rather be described as a *focus*, in time and
in space, for the objective worship of Christ as our
sacrifice. What is in time and in space is not Christ,
but the sacrament ; but the sacrament is so intimately related to Christ that He may rightly and
intelligibly be worshipped *sub specie sacramenti*.
According to the theory of Mr. Spens, it is precisely
because the devout reception of them unites us to
Christ—it is *upon the ground of* the new significance,
capacity, and efficacy which from henceforth attaches,
by Christ's appointment, to the consecrated elements

[1] *Op. cit.*, p. 442.

in virtue of their consecration—that they can rightly be called His Body and His Blood. They set forth to us Christ as our sacrifice, as the Lamb slain from the foundation of the world : and no other conceivable focus in time and in space for the objective adoration of Christ as our sacrifice could possibly be more appropriate, more intimate, or (for some temperaments at least) more inevitable.

There are many persons, moreover, who, accepting this view, will not be disposed to dissent from Mr. Spens' further argument, that, since the Reserved Sacrament is capable of giving communion, and is in no way *in principle* separable (except in time) from the sacrament as given in the course of the liturgy, the same arguments with regard to adoration apply also in this case. ' The devotional use of the Reserved Sacrament is not something independent of Communion and deriving from some separate conception.'[1]

The desirability or otherwise of the devotional use of the Reserved Sacrament is a different question, with regard to which differing opinions are held. The present discipline of the Church of England may not officially countenance it ; but it cannot, upon the basis of the line of argument which has been developed above, be simply excluded as being, of necessity, illegitimate in principle.

[1] Spens, *op. cit.*, p. 445.

On the other hand, is there anything in the type of theology in question which must be pronounced to be unevangelical ?   It is certainly not ' magical ', and it appears to be grounded in the faith of the Gospel.   Is it, in fact, too optimistic to hope that, along the lines indicated, there may be already in sight, so far as the theoretical theology of the Eucharist is concerned, the possibility of a genuine irenicon in principle between reasonable Evangelicals and some, at least, of the representatives of Anglo-Catholicism in the coming generation ?

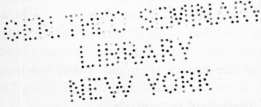
MADE AND PRINTED IN GREAT BRITAIN
AT THE BOWERING PRESS, PLYMOUTH